Life in the Vineyard

Receive · Rejoice · Release

Marcel Sanchez

Life in the Vineyard

Receive - Rejoice - Release

Printed in the United States of America
Kindle Direct Publishing
ISBN: 9781796449297

Cover and interior designed by Brenda Ulloa: Brenda@GlobalChurch.me

Table of Contents

Preface

The Christian life is about a person, Jesus Christ. Jesus is the source of life and the author of the Christian faith (John 1:1-4). The focus of our faith is on a life-giving relationship that grows by faith. Everything around us, and I do mean everything, will attack this life-giving relationship.

What I would like to share with you over the next 30 days is how God has used a simple metaphor to help us understand the simplicity of the Christian life. Whether you've trusted Jesus Christ as Savior just a few minutes ago or you have known Him for more than 30 years, everything you need to live the Christian life still flows from the presence of Christ within you.

I would like to thank a few key people who have made this booklet a reality. My dear friend, Pastor Bud McCord, has invested countless hours in helping to simplify this message. His thoughts are shared throughout this booklet under "Abiding Thoughts" and will serve to help you learn how to live an abiding life. Pastor Bud has trained several Abiding Life Coaches, of which I serve as one. His words of wisdom, expressed throughout these pages are priceless.

Russell Johnson, my friend and Senior Pastor, has provided much wisdom during the entire process. Brenda Ulloa, my very talented sister in Christ, has formatted and designed this work, while lending her expertise to this project.

Last but certainly not least, my beautiful wife, Yami. She has supported me from day one on this project. She also serves as the primary recipient of God's fruit through my life.

Marcel Sanchez

Global Church
17701 NW 57th Avenue
Miami, FL 33055
Office: 305.620.5111, ext. 226
Direct: 786-554-0312

Executive Pastor, Global Church
Marcel@GlobalChurch.me | www.GlobalChurch.me

Founder, Imagine Mobile Church
info@ImagineMobileChurch.com | www.ImagineMobileChurch.com

Congratulations!

Welcome to the Christian Life! It's time to celebrate. You're now a child of the King. Your decision to accept and follow Jesus Christ means that right now, you are a new creation, a new person. You are not the same anymore.

Therefore, if anyone is in Christ, he is a new creation; old things have passed away; behold, all things have become new. (2 Corinthians 5:17)

Simply put, you have been permanently transformed. Your spiritual transformation takes place immediately but the life-application of this change is a moment by moment process. The Christian life is about a person, Jesus Christ, not a program. Jesus produced life-change. Since Jesus lives within you, you already have the entire Christian life available 24X7.

You don't have a shortage of spiritual resources. You don't have a shortage of love, joy, peace, longsuffering, kindness, goodness, faithfulness or self-control. You already possess everything necessary to live the abundant life God intended for you to live. You were designed to live through the vine, Jesus.

This booklet is designed to help you grow in this new relationship during the first 30 days of your life as a believer. If you're already a believer but have taken a spiritual detour from God's purpose for your life, this booklet will help you get back on track. It is designed to help you focus on the priority of the Christian life—Jesus. So don't stress. The purpose of this booklet is to help simplify your life rather than complicate it. In the Christian life, less is more.

Welcome to the Christian life!

To get started, these studies are designed to help you answer three simple, yet profound, questions about the Christian life.

What is the Christian life?

Where is the Christian life?

Why the Christian life?

Big Implications!

These are simple questions with huge implications for our joy and our ability to love like Jesus loved. The answers to these questions will either keep your Christian life simple or complex. Simple is good!

Complex is a burden we want to help you avoid. Getting started right in your new Christian life means starting with Jesus and staying with Jesus. He is the Christian life!

Each of these studies is designed to simplify your life, not confuse it or burden it. Remember, in real Christian life "Simple is good and love is the goal". Consider the effort you will put into these studies as an investment in joy and love.

That's right. When your joy is full, you will be the most like Jesus and you will love people like Jesus loved people. When you are filled with His joy, you will naturally love like Jesus loved. Joy is good for us and good for others.

These words I have spoken to you, that My joy may remain in you, and that your joy may be full. This is My commandment that you love one another as I have loved you. (John 15:11-12)

Can you see the connection between Jesus' joy, your joy, and your ability to love others? The connection is present and available for you right now. Together we will see how this can be our moment by moment reality. Imagine yourself filled with His joy moment by moment. Imagine living a life characterized by complete satisfaction and overflowing abundance.

I have come that they may have life, and that they may have it more abundantly. (John 10:10)

Imagine yourself being able to love without any interruptions. Through these studies, let us help you enjoy Jesus and enjoy loving like Jesus loved others. Your joy and your love is our goal for God's glory!

John 15:1-11

"I am the true vine, and My Father is the vinedresser.
Every branch in Me that does not bear fruit He takes away;
and every branch that bears fruit He prunes, that it may bear more
fruit. You are already clean because of the word which I have spoken
to you. Abide in Me, and I in you. As the branch cannot bear fruit of
itself, unless it abides in the vine, neither can you, unless you abide in
Me. I am the vine, you are the branches. He who abides in Me,
and I in him, bears much fruit; for without Me you can do nothing.
If anyone does not abide in Me, he is cast out as a branch and is
withered; and they gather them and throw them into the fire, and
they are burned. If you abide in Me, and My words abide in you, you
will ask what you desire, and it shall be done for you. By this My Father
is glorified, that you bear much fruit; so you will be My disciples.
As the Father loved Me, I also have loved you; abide in My love.
If you keep My commandments, you will abide in My love,
just as I have kept My Father's commandments and abide in His love.
These things I have spoken to you, that My joy may remain in you,
and that your joy may be full."

Read through John 15:1-11 several times
and write down a few observations regarding
the role of the vinedresser, the vine, and the branches.

_____
_____
_____
_____
_____
_____
_____
_____
_____
_____
_____
_____

A Quick Review: How do I Become a Christian?

Jesus invites you to know him personally. Jesus is a relational Savior. He extends a personal invitation for you to know him. His desire for you is to experience his satisfying life as you remain in his presence. But it's not all about you. Jesus wants you to know him and make him known.

There's an eternal purpose for this relationship. It's not about your personal happiness or particular preferences. There's a divine purpose working through our lives for God's glory. Therefore, Jesus wants his life to flow through your life to those around you. Before living for Jesus you first need to know him personally.

Throughout the course of our study, we will use the word Christian, disciple, and believer interchangeably to describe someone who has a personal relationship with Jesus and is growing spiritually. So let's begin.

Are you a Christian? How do you know? There are many misconceptions about how a person becomes a Christian. With more information available and accessible in our world than ever before in history, it is no wonder why someone can be confused or even misguided by what they have read or have been taught by others.

> For the wages of sin is death, but the free gift of God is eternal life in Christ Jesus our Lord. (Romans 6:23)

Here are a few examples of very sincere, but misguided assumptions about the Christian faith:

"I am a Christian if I go to church regularly.
I am a Christian if I help others.
I am a Christian if I give money to the church or to the poor.
I am a Christian if I read the Bible.
If my parents are Christians, it automatically makes me a Christian.
Since I believe in God, I am a Christian.
I am a Christian because I am a good person."

What were some of your faulty assumptions? Can you think of other misguided assumptions used by close friends or family members?

> As it is written: "None is righteous, no, not one."
> (Romans 3:10)

The Christian life is about a growing relationship with Jesus Christ. Loving, knowing, and serving Jesus is what the Christian life is all about. Jesus is the Christian life. Since God is relational, the Christian life is relational as well. When you begin a relationship with Jesus, you begin a relationship with the Father. You must accept Jesus by faith to truly know him. God's invitation is for everyone in the world and for you personally.

We must recognize that God is holy and just. He's created us in love, but we have willfully rebelled and sinned against Him. Our sin eternally separates us from God. Therefore, we are deserving of His full wrath and judgment because of our sin. The good news is that Jesus Christ came as our substitute, to receive the penalty for our sin. Jesus died for us. His death on the cross satisfied God's wrath and payment for our sins.

Every Invitation Requires a Personal Response

God provided a way for us to be reconciled to Him through the death, burial, and resurrection of Jesus. Today, we can connect with God by grace through faith in Jesus Christ. This is God's invitation for us. What is our response? We are to respond to what God has done through Christ by faith. We must confess our sins, repent, and trust in Jesus.

Since God is relational, the Christian life is relational as well.

If you have never accepted his invitation, are you ready now to begin a vibrant relationship with the God who loves you and died on a cross to give you eternal life?

Now there was a man of the Pharisees named Nicodemus, a ruler of the Jews. This man came to Jesus by night and said to him, "Rabbi, we know that you are a teacher come from God, for no one can do these signs that you do unless God is with him." Jesus answered him, "Truly, truly, I say to you, unless one is born again he cannot see the kingdom of God." Nicodemus said to him, "How can a man be born when he is old? Can he enter a second time into his mother's womb and be born?" Jesus answered, "Truly, truly, I say to you, unless one is born of water and the Spirit, he cannot enter the kingdom of God. That which is born of the flesh is flesh, and that which is born of the Spirit is spirit." (John 3:1-6)

Let's review the steps involved for becoming a Christian. This is a great reminder and a tool for you to use as you share your faith with others. Here are four key words to guide you: God, sin, Jesus and connection.

God: God loves YOU! Recognize that He loves you just the way you are, unconditionally. His desire is for you to know Him. God wants you to find complete spiritual satisfaction by starting a vibrant relationship with His Son, Jesus Christ.

> For God so loved the world that He gave His only begotten Son, that whoever believes in Him should not perish but have everlasting life.
> (John 3:16)

Sin: Know and admit that your SIN has separated you from God. Knowingly or unknowingly you've broken one of God's Ten Commandments, his standard for perfection. Right now, you stand guilty before God for your sin.

> For all have sinned and fall short of the glory of God. (Romans 3:23)

Your personal goodness or ability to help others can't solve the separation problem. There is NOTHING you can do to pay for the penalty of your sins. Morality, religion, generosity, or good works do not satisfy God's perfect standard.

> There is a way that seems right to a man, but its end is the way of death.
> (Proverbs 14:12)

> "Now faith is the assurance of things hoped for, the conviction of things not seen." (Hebrews 11:1, NASB)

> For the wages of sin is death, but the free gift of God is eternal life in Christ Jesus our Lord. (Romans 6:23)

> And just as it is appointed for man to die once, and after that comes judgment. (Hebrews 9:27)

Jesus: Jesus died on the cross to pay for the penalty of your sins.
He is God's ONLY solution to your sin problem. Jesus died on the cross to connect you to God. Jesus was buried and on the third day, he rose from the grave. Jesus is the Mediator between God and man. There is no other. Jesus was your substitute, and his death paid the penalty of your sins.

For Christ also suffered once for sins, the just for the unjust,
that He might bring us to God. (1 Peter 3:18)

Jesus said to him, "I am the way, the truth, and the life.
No one comes to the Father except through Me. (John 14:6)

Connection: Believing, confessing, and receiving. You connect with God through FAITH, by believing in Jesus' finished work on the cross and confessing your sins directly to Him through prayer. You receive Jesus by personal invitation.

But as many as received Him, to them He gave the right to become
children of God, to those who believe in His name. (John 1:12)

If we confess our sins, He is faithful and just to forgive us our sins
and to cleanse us from all unrighteousness. (1 John 1:9)

If you confess with your mouth the Lord Jesus and believe in your heart
that God has raised Him from the dead, you will be saved. (Romans 10:9)

Starting the Christian Life: You begin the Christian life through a prayer of faith. What pleases God is our faith. Here is a sample prayer to repeat out loud to the Lord...

Lord God, I thank You for Your great love for me. Today I understand how much You love me. I know that I have sinned against You and broken your commandments. I'm truly sorry. I ask you, Lord Jesus, to forgive me for all my sins. Cleanse my heart and make all things new. Jesus, I believe that you died on the cross to pay for my sins. I believe that you were buried and on the third day, you rose again from the grave. Today I invite you into my heart and receive you as Lord and Savior. Amen.

Living Through Your Identity in Christ

You are loved by God. It is very important for us to understand how God sees us at this very moment in Christ Jesus. Secondly, it is important for us to see ourselves as God sees us. The first profound truth we need to embrace is the following: we are loved by God; you are loved by God (Ephesians 1:4).

You are a work of God; created in Christ Jesus for good works.

God loved you before he created the earth. God loves you with a perfect love. His love for you is beyond measure. It is eternal, perfect, and abounding in mercy and grace.

God's love called us out of darkness and into the light through Jesus Christ. In Christ, we have direct access to the Father. Our conversations with God are personal and relational. God created us in his image, blessed us with every spiritual blessing in Christ, and redeemed us from the penalty of our sins. God promises to never leave us. He protects us from evil, leads us through difficulties, and provides us with more grace as we have need.

Yet in all these things we are more than conquerors through Him who loved us. For I am persuaded that neither death nor life, nor angels nor principalities nor powers, nor things present nor things to come, nor height nor depth, nor any other created thing shall be able to separate us from the love of God which is in Christ Jesus our Lord. (Romans 8:37-39)

Read each statement about our identity in Christ out loud, starting with the simple phrase, "I am".

"I am...

Created in God's Image (Genesis 1:27)
Loved by God (John 3:16)
Inseparable from God (Romans 8:37-39)
Chosen (Ephesians 1:4)
Blameless (Ephesians 1:4)
Predestined (Ephesians 1:11)
Forgiven (Colossians 1:13-14)
Complete in Jesus (Colossians 2:10)

Known by God (Jeremiah 1:5)
Christ's Friend (John 15:15)
In Christ (Galatians 2:20)
Holy (Ephesians 1:4)
Redeemed (Ephesians 1:7)
Provided for (Philippians 4:19)
Loved (Colossians 3:12)
Chosen by God (1 Peter 2:9)

You belong to God's family

God is relational. He has always existed in perfect relationship with Jesus and the Holy Spirit. God designed for people, working through families, to reach all people groups and nations of the earth. Working through family relationships has been a part of his plan all along.

> For he chose us in him before the creation of the world to be holy
> and blameless in his sight. In love. (Ephesians 1:4, NIV)

God brought you into his family through Christ Jesus. You are a part of an eternal family, a living body of believers from all nations, tribes, and tongues. Being a part of God's family is a very special privilege. We are sons and daughters of the King of Kings and Lord of Lords, Jesus.

> The Spirit Himself testifies together with our spirit that we are God's children.
> (Romans 8:16, HCSB)

I am...

Rightfully God's Child (John 1:12)
Reigning with Christ (Romans 5:17)
Part of Christ's Body (1 Corinthians 12:27)
Purchased by Christ (1 Corinthians 6:20)
Established by God (2 Corinthians 1:21)
A Spiritual Family in Christ (Galatians 3:28)
A Member of Christ's Body (Ephesians 3:6)
A Partaker of His Promise (Ephesians 3:6)
A Partaker of Divine Nature (2 Peter 1:4)

Chosen (John 15:16)
A Child of God (Rom. 8:16)
God's Property (Eph. 1:11)

> This mystery is that through the gospel the Gentiles are heirs together with Israel,
> members together of one body, and sharers together in the promise
> in Christ Jesus. (Ephesians 3:6, NIV)

> But God, who is rich in mercy, because of His great love with which He loved us,
> even when we were dead in trespasses, made us alive together with Christ
> (by grace you have been saved). (Ephesians 2:4-5, NKJV)

> We know that our old self was crucified with him in order that the body of sin might
> be brought to nothing so that we would no longer be enslaved to sin. For one who
> has died has been set free from sin. Now if we have died with Christ, we believe
> that we will also live with him. (Romans 6:6-8)

You have been redeemed through Christ

Spiritual redemption has to do with paying off a debt in full. The debt is ours alone. When Jesus died on the cross to pay for the penalty of our sins, he paid our debt completely with his own blood. As a result, we are God's children by grace through faith in Jesus Christ. His perfect work on the cross was the only way to buy us back from sin and death and into God's kingdom.

In him we have redemption through his blood, the forgiveness of sins, in accordance with the riches of God's grace. (Ephesians 1:7, NIV)

In Christ, we now have peace with God, justification, sanctification, adoption as his children, and eternal security. We have been crucified with Christ. Our old life is dead. We now live for Jesus. Remember, even though our salvation is free, it was extremely costly.

I am...

A Saint (Romans 1:7)
At Peace with God (Romans 5:1)
Crucified with Jesus (Romans 6:6-8)
No Longer Blind (2 Corinthians 3:14)
Saved by Grace (Ephesians 2:4-5)
Washed (1 Corinthians 6:11)
Brought Near by Christ's Blood (Ephesians 2:13)

Justified (Romans 3:24)
Saved Forever (Romans 5:9-10)
Reconciled (Romans 5:11)
Redeemed (Galatians 3:13)
Alive in Christ (Ephesians 2:4-5)
Sanctified (1 Corinthians 6:11)

Or do you not know that your body is a temple of the Holy Spirit who is in you, whom you have from God, and that you are not your own? For you have been bought with a price: therefore glorify God in your body.
(1 Corinthians 6:19 - 20, NASB)

When you heard the message of truth, the gospel of your salvation, and when you believed in Him, you were also sealed with the promised Holy Spirit.
(Ephesians 1:13, HCSB)

You did not choose Me but I chose you, and appointed you that you would go and bear fruit, and that your fruit would remain, so that whatever you ask of the Father in My name He may give to you. (John 15:16, NASB)

You are holy; set apart and free from sin

Our identity is established in holiness. God is holy. He commands us to pursue holiness in all matters of life. Our conduct is to be counter-cultural when the culture follows an unbiblical path. Jesus gives us a new way to follow.

When it comes to sin, our lives should be spotless, blameless, and without a hint of deception. We are free from sin and no longer enslaved to its rule over our lives (Romans 6:6-8). We now live from our identity in Christ Jesus. We are slaves to Christ alone.

In Christ we are holy, set apart by God and for God's purposes. Our thoughts, words, attitudes, and actions should mirror God's standard for holiness. God makes us holy. We belong to him. We are alive to God and dead to sin (Romans 6:8-11). We have been set free from sin's power, so let's start living in Christ's freedom.

I am...

Free in Christ (John 8:36)
Dead to Sin (Romans 6:11)
Free from Sin and Death (Romans 8:2)
Washed (1 Corinthians 6:11)
God's Temple (1 Corinthians 6:19)
Set Free in Christ (Galatians 5:1)
No Longer Sin's Slave (Galatians 4:7)

Free from Sin (Romans 6:6-8)
Alive to God (Romans 6:11)
God's Temple (Romans 8:11)
Sanctified (1 Corinthians 6:11)
Set Apart (1 Corinthians 1:2)
Holy (1 Peter 2:9)

Yet in all these things we are more than conquerors through Him who loved us. For I am persuaded that neither death nor life, nor angels nor principalities nor powers, nor things present nor things to come, nor height nor depth, nor any other created thing, shall be able to separate us from the love of God which is in Christ Jesus our Lord. (Romans 8:37-39)

There is therefore now no condemnation to those who are in Christ Jesus, who do not walk according to the flesh, but according to the Spirit. (Romans 8:1, NKJV)

You are eternally secure in Christ

One of the challenges many believers struggle through is the doctrine of eternal security. In Christ we are secure, forever (Romans 8:31-39). We will always belong to the Lord our God. The Holy Spirit guarantees our salvation. He sealed us with Christ and raised us with Christ.

We no longer have to worry about condemnation. There is no condemnation for those who are in Christ Jesus (Romans 8:1). When we sin we can seek God's mercy. We don't have to wonder if God will forgive us; we can know with certainty (1 John 1:9-10).

As citizens of heaven, God is preparing a place for us. We are already sealed in Heaven with Christ. We already reign with Christ. We are united in Christ. And let's not forget, we are forever united with Christ. Spiritual insecurity comes when our thinking or our emotions do not align with what the Bible says about our present or our future. We can rest in God's Word. God accepts us on the basis of his great love and grace.

I am...

Free from Condemnation (Romans 8:1)
Free from Sin and Death (Romans 8:2)
A Joint Heir with Christ (Romans 8:17)
Accepted by Christ (Romans 15:7)
United with Christ (1 Corinthians 6:17)
Clothed with Christ (Galatians 3:27)
Hidden with Christ in God (Col. 3:3)
Seated in Heaven with Christ (Eph. 2:6)

One in Christ (John 17:20-21)
Secure (Romans 8:31-39)
Acceptable to God (Rom. 14:18)
Raised with Christ (Colossians 3:1)
One Spirit with Christ (1 Cor. 6:17)
Sealed with Christ (Eph. 1:13)
A Citizen of Heaven (Phil. 3:20)

For He rescued us from the domain of darkness, and transferred us to the kingdom of His beloved Son, in whom we have redemption, the forgiveness of sins.
(Colossians 1:13-14)

Praise be to the God and Father of our Lord Jesus Christ, who has blessed us in the heavenly realms with every spiritual blessing in Christ. (Ephesians 1:3, NIV)

You are complete in Christ

Our sufficiency comes from God and God alone. If we have Jesus, we have enough, more than enough. One of the mistakes believers make is to pursue experiences rather than Jesus. They seek to develop unintelligible languages, bizarre spiritual encounters, and other experiences to "complete them" and make them "whole" in some way. And for those who have supposedly "found" these experiences, they spend much of their energy trying to convince other believers of what they're missing.

This sad reality is all too common these days. God's Word is perfect in every way. We are to measure every voice, spirit, and experience through the grid of God's holy Word. And for our spiritual stability, let's stop searching for more. We have Christ and Christ is enough. We have been immersed into Christ through salvation (Galatians 3:27).

We have Christ and Christ is enough.

We have the fullness of Christ living within us. We are complete in Christ and Christ alone. We don't need another person, experience, possession or purchase to complete us. Christ is our sufficiency. Christ is the one who completes us and makes us whole. We lack nothing.

I am...

Resurrected (Romans 6:9-11)   A Conqueror (Romans 8:37)
Triumphant in Christ (2 Cor. 2:14)   A New Creation (2 Cor. 5:17)
Baptized into Christ (Galatians 3:27)   Righteous (Ephesians 4:24)
Complete in Christ (Colossians 2:10)
Blessed with Every Spiritual Blessing (Ephesians 1:13)

Now thanks be to God who always leads us in triumph in Christ,
and through us diffuses the fragrance of His knowledge in every place.
(2 Corinthians 2:14, NKJV)

But thanks be to God, who in Christ always leads us in triumphal procession,
and through us spreads the fragrance of the knowledge of him everywhere.
(2 Corinthians 2:14)

You have a new purpose

Part of understanding our new identity in Christ Jesus means having a much clearer picture of our purpose in life. We have a future purpose and a present purpose to live out. We are no longer a prisoner of our past. The past is past and the future is ahead of us. In Christ, we have a future and a living hope! God's Word provides us with everything needed to live a vibrant Christian life. Our future has been secured by God's unchanging love (Romans 8:37-39).

We are reminded of our purpose in John's Gospel as the Lord Jesus asked Simon Peter to feed his sheep twice in the conversation.

"He said to him the third time, 'Simon, son of Jonah, do you love Me' Peter was grieved because He said to him the third time, 'Do you love Me?' And he said to Him, 'Lord, You know all things, You know that I love You.' Jesus said to him, 'Feed My sheep'. . .And when He had spoken this, He said to him, 'Follow Me'" (John 21:17 - 18, NKJV).

Our new purpose involves equipping God's people for works of service. We do this with every skill, gift, talent, ability, and experience we have. We do this to advance God's kingdom. We do this to make disciples and multiply God's work. We do these things because of who we are as sons and daughters of the Eternal King. Our identity in Christ compels us to equip others for Christ. This is our responsibility; this is our divine calling.

I am...

A Branch of the True Vine (John 15:1-8)   Salt and Light (Matthew 5:13)
Chosen to Bear Fruit (John 15:16)   Christ's Instrument (Rom. 15:18)
The Righteousness of God (2 Cor. 5:21)   A Work of God (Eph. 2:10)

You did not choose Me but I chose you, and appointed you that you would go and bear fruit, and that your fruit would remain, so that whatever you ask of the Father in My name He may give to you. (John 15:16, NASB)

For we are God's handiwork, created in Christ Jesus to do good works, which God prepared in advance for us to do. (Ephesians 2:10, NIV)

You have a new mission

After God's Spirit worked through his personal prejudices, the Apostle Peter concluded,

"In truth I perceive that God shows no partiality. But in every nation whoever fears Him and works righteousness is accepted by Him. . .whoever believes in Him will receive remission of sins." (Acts 10:34-35, 43)

Here is where we understand the infinite value placed by God on all peoples, from every nation, tongue, and tribe. God is a global God. His vision and mission is to reach the whole world. As with many, our identity has changed from a local perspective to a global focus.

I am...

Created for Good Works (Eph. 2:10)
Confident in My Access to God (Eph. 3:12)
Called to Declare God's Praises (1 Peter 2:9)

Bold (Ephesians 3:12)
Light (Ephesians 5:8)
A Royal Priest (1 Peter 2:9)

Besides this I have:

Complete Satisfaction in Christ
The Holy Spirit
Life in God
The Mind of Christ
The Promises of God

Direct access to the Father
Eternal Security in Christ Jesus
An Eternal Purpose
A perfect life for me—Jesus
A perfect life in me—Jesus

We are therefore Christ's ambassadors, as though God were making his appeal through us. We implore you on Christ's behalf: Be reconciled to God. God made him who had no sin to be sin for us, so that in him we might become the righteousness of God. (2 Corinthians 5:20 - 21)

In him and through faith in him we may approach God with freedom and confidence. (Ephesians 3:12, NIV)

And a voice spoke to him again the second time, 'What God has cleansed you must not call common.' This was done three times. . . (Acts 10:15 - 16, NKJV)

Memory Verses to Know

Write the following memory verses on a flashcard. Take 10 minutes each day and review these verses out loud. These verses will encourage you and give you the tools needed to share God's work in your life with someone else.

"I am the vine, you are the branches. He who abides in Me, and I in him, bears much fruit; for without Me you can do nothing." (John 15:5)

"I have been crucified with Christ; it is no longer I who live, but Christ lives in me; and the life which I now live in the flesh I live by faith in the Son of God, who loved me and gave Himself for me." (Galatians 2:20)

"For God so loved the world that He gave His only begotten Son, that whoever believes in Him should not perish but have everlasting life." (John 3:16)

"For all have sinned and fall short of the glory of God." (Romans 3:23)

"For Christ also suffered once for sins, the just for the unjust, that He might bring us to God." (1 Peter 3:18)

"Jesus said to him, 'I am the way, the truth, and the life. No one comes to the Father except through Me.'" (John 14:6)

"If we confess our sins, He is faithful and just to forgive us our sins and to cleanse us from all unrighteousness." (1 John 1:9)

"If you confess with your mouth the Lord Jesus and believe in your heart that God has raised Him from the dead, you will be saved." (Romans 10:9)

Terms to Understand:

Receive: Actively listening and drawing what is needed to live the Christian life from the source of life, Jesus. He is the vine and you're His precious branch.

Rejoice: Reflecting on the goodness of God, the vinedresser, and considering how His instructions can flow through every area of your life.

Release: Taking what you have received from the vine and intentionally delivering this fruit to those who need it most. You were designed to deliver.

Day #1 - A New Source for Satisfaction

I am the true vine. (John 15:1)

New products can be both exciting and dangerous. They often represent the latest trends in the market. It may be a new software program, a great tool, or the latest personal gadget. Sometimes these products can replace what we have used for years. They have an enormous potential to disrupt the way we think and even our way of life, for the better or for the worse. But no product can ever satisfy our soul. Only God can satisfy the soul. Only God can completely quench the spiritual thirst we all have for eternity and significance. Through his Son, Jesus, God satisfies the soul.

God extends spiritual satisfaction and eternal life exclusively, through His Son, Jesus.

God is the source of all wisdom and spiritual satisfaction (John 15:1). Starting with Abraham, God planted the nation of Israel as a vine with the intent to make God known and visible to the entire world. God's desire was to connect all people to Himself through the nation of Israel. Israel failed repeatedly as a nation by disobeying God's Word and by extension, producing bad fruit:

Yet I planted you a choice vine, wholly of pure seed. How then have you turned degenerate and become a wild vine? (Jeremiah 2:21)

God's heart has not changed. He still wants to connect people from all ethnic groups to Himself. God loves the entire world. God loves you. He still wants to produce something special, something with an eternal impact through your life. Today, however, God extends spiritual satisfaction and eternal life exclusively through His Son, Jesus. The Lord Jesus, the true vine, connects us to God. Jesus is the source.

I am the way, the truth, and the life. No one comes to the Father except through Me. (John 14:6)

Jesus is eternal life. He is the living vine. Before you took your first breath, Jesus was intimately involved in the creation and fulfillment of God's plan for your life. You discover your purpose for living as you remain in the source of life, Jesus Christ. He knows you better than you know yourself. When we drift and look for life or significance from other sources, he will remind you who is the true source of life. You have been connected to the Life to deliver life. What a high honor! What a great privilege!

You've been connected to the vine to deliver a continuous flow of love to others. As a branch, you already have all that you need to do what God wants to accomplish through your life. You do not lack anything! You are complete in Christ. Christ is enough; He is sufficient and you are complete in Him. You are now a conduit of God's grace. As the true vine, Jesus connects you to the Father, the vinedresser, and provides what is needed to make God known and clearly visible to those who don't yet know Him.

You have been connected to the Life to deliver life.

Jesus is the true vine and you are His branch. You are not the vine; so don't try to be the vine. You are not the vinedresser; so don't try to be the vinedresser. You are not the root; so don't try to be the root. You are not the leaves; so don't try to be the leaves. You are not the fruit; so don't try to be the fruit. When we confuse our identity, we don't fulfill God's purpose for our lives. Be a good branch. As a branch, receiving a consistent flow of life-changing spiritual nourishment from the vine is your top priority. There is nothing more important for a branch to do.

I am the vine, you are the branches. He who abides in Me, and I in him, bears much fruit; for without Me you can do nothing. (John 15:5)

Receive: Right now, take 10 minutes to thank God in prayer for being your new source of spiritual satisfaction. Ask Him to show you how to stay focused on Jesus. Make it a point to pray every day and begin memorizing John 15:5.

Rejoice: What truth have I learned or been reminded of today?

Release: Who can I share this with today?

Day #2 - The Care of the Vinedresser

I am the true vine and My Father is the vinedresser. (John 15:1)

Grandparents often have a special bond with their grandchildren. This connection is unique. The way they approach their grandchildren can be described with three simple words: love, care, and protection. They lavish these three things on their grandchildren. This relationship can be an important part of children's lives and help them mature in many ways.

God the Father, the vinedresser, loves us with an eternal love. We will never completely comprehend the Father's love on this side of heaven. The Father cares for us deeply. Nothing escapes His perfect knowledge. The Lord knows the exact condition of His branches. He knows when they are doing well and thriving. He is also fully aware when they are not.

The branches are often unaware of the dangers around them and how these threats might affect their relationship to the vine. The branches are limited in knowledge and in strength to protect themselves. The vinedresser protects His branches from danger. As needed, He makes the necessary adjustments to protect His branches. Even if the branches experience temporary discomfort, pain or loss the vinedresser takes swift action to provide for the longterm protection and health of the branches.

As the vinedresser, He is completely and
intimately aware of every detail of your life.

The metaphor of John 15:1-11 will help you understand how the Christian life is supposed to work. God's plan is not complicated; it is simple, very simple. As the vinedresser, He is completely and intimately aware of every detail of your life. God knows what you are doing all of the time. He knows because He genuinely cares. He knows because He loves you.

God is the One who protects,
manages, and cares for the vineyard.

God's love for you is unconditional. His plan for your life is a good one. He is the One who protects, manages, and cares for the vineyard. For this reason, He wants to produce the visible demonstration of His love through your life, as you receive spiritual nourishment from the vine. The vinedresser will make sure that all nourishment flows from the vine to the branches. As His precious branch, make sure you are ready to receive it.

God knows exactly what is needed for the vineyard to thrive and produce healthy fruit. He has a perfect plan ready to flow through your life. He knows what conditions generate the most fruit. Moreover, God knows how to cultivate the right environment for your life to flourish and produce high-quality fruit. His plan for your life will produce much fruit. Let Him care for you and show you the best way. God is very good at doing this.

God already simplified the process for your spiritual growth. Don't stress! Remember, your new source of satisfaction is not found in a program, an experience, an achievement, or in a material possession. Your new source of satisfaction is found in a person, Jesus Christ. He is the source of life.

Thank God for the work He has started and the fruit He will produce through your life. It takes time to get to know the vinedresser. God loves you. He truly cares for you. God will protect you and help mature you.

God knows how to cultivate the right environment
for your life to flourish and produce good fruit.

Receive: Spend the bulk of your time today thanking God for His great power, protection, and care for your life. Thank Him for the work He has started and the fruit He will produce through you. Start reading one chapter a day from the Gospel of John. Continue memorizing John 15:5.

Rejoice: Prayerfully consider the following: When was the last time I thanked God for His great power, protection, and care over my life?

Release: As a result of these truths, what might need to change in my attitude, beliefs, and actions? What steps do I need to take outwardly?

Day #3 - From the Inside Out

If anyone thirsts, let him come to Me and drink. He who believes in Me, as the Scripture has said, out of his heart will flow rivers of living water. (John 7:37 - 38)

Good wells provide an unlimited source of water. In ancient times, wells also served as social landmarks. There were certain times of the day when people would gather, talk, and draw water from the well. Since water was a daily need, relationships were often started and developed at the well. Jesus reached the entire town of Sychar by starting a simple conversation about water with a woman at Jacob's well (John 4:1-42). This woman came searching for physical water and left with living water.

Temporary satisfaction from thirst was found at the well. The water at the well was insufficient to permanently satisfy our need for ongoing water. Jesus used water as an illustration to explain his power to permanently satisfy our spiritual thirst and produce a spring of living water which never ends.

Your search is over! As a believer, your complete spiritual satisfaction is already living within you—forever. Jesus Christ, the true vine, is also the only one who can quench your spiritual thirst. Now you can rest. Your spirit has finally found what it's been searching for. Jesus, the Eternal God, now lives within you.

> Your complete spiritual satisfaction
> is already living within you—forever.

God's Spirit is ready to flow through your life like a rushing, mighty river. As you increase the receiving, God can increase the flowing. You are now designed to deliver life from the inside out. In Christ, your life is a conduit of life for others! For this reason, you must allow His life to freely flow through you to others.

> Your life is designed to deliver life from the inside out.

Recognize that you are no longer the one living. Your "old self" was crucified with Christ. The "old you" is gone and the "new you" in Christ Jesus is here to stay. Christ lives within you, and works through your life to deliver life to others. Notice how Paul explains this new spiritual reality:

I have been crucified with Christ; it is no longer I who live, but Christ lives in me; and the life which I now live in the flesh I live by faith in the Son of God, who loved me and gave Himself for me. (Galatians 2:20)

Jesus Christ paid for your sins with His own blood as He died on the cross. Your life does not belong to you any longer. In Christ Jesus, you are God's property, His very own special treasure; you belong to the Living God. Your body belongs to God; your property and money belongs to God; your career and plans belong to God; and your relationships belong to God. Since Jesus is the Lord of your life, He is the one in charge.

As you learn to receive a constant flow of spiritual nourishment from the vine, your life will be characterized by faith—one that trusts the vinedresser in every situation. You can't receive from the vine or please the vinedresser without faith. The vinedresser will often allow you to enter into a situation to test your faith. You don't have to fear when God gives you a test. He wants to test whether or not you will trust Him and follow his Word or trust yourself and follow your own understanding to finish the test.

Did you know that your faith is a visible demonstration of your love for God? Faith is an unshakable trust in God that moves us to take action. Your faith is revealed through your works of service to God, His church, and through your service to others. As God changes you from the inside out, your faith will grow and your good works will increase. What God wants to give you is received by faith and what God wants you to give others is delivered and practiced by faith.

Faith is an unshakable trust in God that moves us to take action.

Receive: Open your Bible and read Hebrews 11:6. Continue memorizing John 15:5 and add Galatians 2:20 to your list.

Rejoice: Prayerfully consider the following: Am I regularly allowing God to change me from the inside out and serve others in the process?

Release: What have you pursued in the past to quench your spiritual thirst? What areas of temporary satisfaction has the Lord helped you overcome? What might need to change in your attitude, beliefs, and actions?

Day #4 - A False Connection

Every branch in Me that does not bear fruit He takes away. (John 15:2)

Experienced electricians know the importance of establishing good connections when joining electrical wires together. They also know the potential hazards when inexperienced workers perform these connections. Faulty connections are dangerous. Property can be significantly damaged or destroyed. People can get severely hurt; some may lose their lives as a result of these problems. Short circuits, fires, and even explosions can result when faulty connections are made. Knowledgeable electricians will make the right connections.

> Your purpose as a branch is to bear fruit—to make God visible to others by allowing the qualities of God to continuously flow through your life.

Not every branch is rightly connected. Just because someone says, "I'm a branch," does not automatically make him or her a branch. Some branches are rightly connected to the vine, and others are not. On the outside, some branches may look, feel, and even smell like other healthy branches. Unless you're a vinedresser or a skilled gardener, you wouldn't easily notice the difference. This can be difficult to see. Similarly, some people who call themselves Christians are rightly connected to the vine, and others are not.

> Not every branch is rightly connected to the vine.

Those who aren't may say the right things, regularly attend church services, and even volunteer their time. You wouldn't notice the difference either, at least not immediately. The book of First John makes it clear; we can identify a true believer by the fruit of their life. The fruit of your life points to the source of your life. Spiritual fruit flows from spiritual transformation. A changed life is produced from a changed heart through the power of the Holy Spirit. Your purpose as a branch is to bear fruit—to make God visible to others by allowing the qualities of God to continuously flow through your life. John explains the difference:

God is light and in Him is no darkness at all. If we say that we have fellowship with Him, and walk in darkness, we lie and do not practice the truth. But if we walk in the light as He is in the light, we have fellowship with one another, and the blood of Jesus Christ His Son cleanses us from all sin. (1 John 1:5,7)

Someone who claims to be a Christian, a follower of Jesus, but who does not produce fruit, is not really a true believer. Every branch that is truly connected to the vine will produce fruit. What we practice in life, through our motives, words, and actions, gives evidence to our true source. Every true Christian produces fruit, even if in very small amounts. When you are rightly connected to the vine, your life will change, and you will make God's presence visible to a dying world by producing fruit.

Spiritual fruit flows from spiritual transformation.

God created you to produce good spiritual fruit. He created you to live in the light by trusting in the Lord and following God's Word. Every true Christian is rightly connected in Christ. With this in mind, avoid false connections. Avoid people who speak spiritual words and claim to be followers of Jesus, but regularly practice carnal attitudes and actions.

Beware of false prophets, who come to you in sheep's clothing but inwardly are ravenous wolves. You will recognize them by their fruits. Are grapes gathered from thornbushes, or figs from thistles? So, every healthy tree bears good fruit, but the diseased tree bears bad fruit. A healthy tree cannot bear bad fruit, nor can a diseased tree bear good fruit. Every tree that does not bear good fruit is cut down and thrown into the fire. Thus you will recognize them by their fruits.
(Matthew 7:15 - 20, ESV)

Receive: Begin memorizing John 3:16 and Romans 3:23. Read First John 1:5-7 several times and spend some time in prayer, asking the Lord to help you walk in the light. Start praying each day for 10-20 minutes.

Rejoice: Prayerfully consider the following: Am I rightly connected to Jesus Christ? Is my life regularly radiating more light than darkness?

Release: Continue reading through the Gospel of John and share what you're learning with others.

Day #5 - Stay Focused

Beware of false prophets, who come to you in sheep's clothing but inwardly are ravenous wolves. You will recognize them by their fruits. Are grapes gathered from thornbushes, or figs from thistles? So, every healthy tree bears good fruit, but the diseased tree bears bad fruit. A healthy tree cannot bear bad fruit, nor can a diseased tree bear good fruit. Every tree that does not bear good fruit is cut down and thrown into the fire. Thus you will recognize them by their fruits. (Matthew 7:15 - 20)

Your letter is almost finished. Your cell phone rings just as you're about to begin writing the last paragraph. You press the ignore button and continue writing. Shortly after, a noisy news helicopter decides to hover over your home to get a better view of the local traffic. Your dog naturally gets frightened and begins to bark for the next thirty minutes. To make matters worse, your neighbor knocks forcefully on your front door to complain about your dog. How can you finish with so many distractions?

In the Christian life there are multitudes of distractions. Sometimes these distractions will demand your full attention. However, as a branch, your primary responsibility is to stay focused on the vine. Daily activities, people, and events work hard to shift your focus from the internal to the external, from the eternal to the temporary, and from the One who truly satisfies to those who can never satisfy. Do not get discouraged by the meaningless activity of other branches; you cannot control their behavior.

As a branch, your primary responsibility
is to stay focused on the vine.

Don't let the behavior or condition of other branches take your focus away from the vine. Keep your full attention on Jesus. The Christian life is sourced through the vine not through other branches. The more you focus on the vine, the more visible God's attributes will be made known to others.

The more you focus on the vine, the more visible God's
attributes will be made known to others.

As you intentionally allow the qualities of God to flow through you, he will produce life through your life. In other words, God is the one who produces spiritual fruit. The good news is that you don't have to produce anything. Really...you don't. You are not supposed to worry about producing fruit. God is the producer. You do, however, have to stay focused on the vine for His life to unreservedly flow through your life.

As you intentionally allow the qualities of God to flow through you, He will produce life through your life.

As a branch, your most critical role is simply to rest and receive from the vine! Jesus is the vine, your daily source for spiritual nourishment. Don't look for this nourishment in other branches, they can't supply it. Don't look for this nourishment in other activities, you won't find it. Don't get distracted and don't get derailed from the simplicity of following Jesus. Jesus is the Christian life. Our focus should rest and remain in Christ alone.

Remember, everything you need to live the Christian life you already have in Jesus Christ. You do not lack anything. He is your source. You live in Christ and Christ lives in you. Like a good soldier, keep advancing and finish God's mission for your life. Stay focused on the vine.

There are many things which can serve to distract us from abiding in Christ. From a practical perspective, staying focused on Christ will reduce the level of anxiety in our lives. Recognizing the sovereignty of God and his absolute power over all things, including people, is essential to remaining in the vine. We cannot control what others say or do, but we can practice self-control in every area of our lives. And yes, we can deliberately make time to focus our attention on our Savior, the True Vine.

Receive: Continue memorizing John 15:5 and Galatians 2:20. Thank God for being your source for spiritual satisfaction. Ask Him to help you remove distractions and stay focused.

Rejoice: Prayerfully consider the following: Am I allowing the temporal things of this life to distract me from the eternal? If so, why?

Release: What has historically distracted me from remaining in the presence of Christ and learning from God's Word? What do I need to adjust in my schedule to stay more focused on the vine?

Abiding Thoughts

Jesus is God's perfection for us and in us.

God demands a perfect life. That perfect life is Jesus.
That perfect life is in me right now.

The difference between Jesus and me is simple.
He was 100% satisfied in God 24 hours a day
and seven days a week, and I am not.

Affirming each day who I am in Christ
motivates me to live accordingly.

Living for God is to enter into the flow of God's intentions
which never change.

I must receive, rejoice and release.
The "source of source" wants to flow through me.

The most important thing I can do to start each day
is to be a great receiver.

Abiding is enjoying a barrier-free relationship with the Vine - Jesus-
and releasing what the Vine wants to give to others through me.

Day #6 - Connected for a Purpose

And every branch that bears fruit... (John 15:2)

As children are growing up they often say, "I can't wait until I'm bigger." This may mean reaching a certain height, weight, or being much older. They want to develop faster than the normal course of life will allow. They believe if they arrive much faster, all will be well and life will be perfect. They want greater challenges and more complex problems to solve.

In the Christian life, spiritual maturity and spiritual fruit take time to develop. We may want to go faster or climb at an accelerated rate, but this is not the way things work in the spiritual arena. We grow progressively as we allow the Holy Spirit to change us into the image of Christ. Each step of maturity will lead us to abide in Christ, practice holiness, take a step of faith and walk in total obedience to God's Word.

The life of a branch is very simple. Your purpose as a branch is to bear fruit—to make God visible to others by allowing the qualities of God to continuously flow through your life. Connections are very important. Having the right connection to the vine is absolutely necessary in the production of spiritual fruit. As a branch, your purpose is to bear much fruit by making God visible to others. This is your primary mission.

The presence of the vinedresser is powerful. A continuous flow of spiritual fruit magnifies God's presence in this world and brings life-transformation to those who are connected to the wrong things. God's presence is the catalyst for eliminating the pain of this world. As Christ's branch, your role is to allow his presence to flow through your life without any obstacles or restrictions.

As a branch, your purpose is to bear fruit
by making God visible to others.

Your spiritual maturity is a progression, not a singular event. Spiritual growth is realized in your uninterrupted connection to the vine and through your consistent delivery of this fruit to others who need it. In the Christian life, your spiritual maturity depends more on your consistency to receive from the vine and release spiritual fruit than it does on any one-time event. Do you see how important it is to receive from Christ today?

Are you making time every day to grow spiritually by abiding in Christ? Remaining in the presence of Christ is foundational to realizing your purpose as a branch. As we spend time with Christ regularly, we learn to apply God's Word in new and exciting ways.

Your spiritual maturity is a progression not a one-time event.

The visible demonstration of God's love, the fruit, is not for you to produce, but to receive, celebrate, and release. As a branch, this is your role. As God's branch, this is your divine purpose. But you may ask, "What does fruit look like?" You may even ask, "How do I know if I am producing the right kind of fruit?" Great questions! Here is just a sample of the fruit you are supposed to deliver to others on a daily basis:

But the fruit of the Spirit is love, joy, peace, longsuffering, kindness, goodness, faithfulness, gentleness, self-control. (Galatians 5:22 - 23)

Receive: Spend some time in prayer, asking the Lord to help you understand your purpose as a branch: receive, rejoice, and release. Thank Him for giving your life a new purpose. Continue studying and memorizing John 3:16 and Romans 3:23. Continue reading one chapter a day from the Gospel of John.

Rejoice: Open your Bible and read Hebrews 12:3. Prayerfully consider the following: Am I choosing to allow discouragement to keep me from fulfilling the purpose God has for me?

Release: Have I been impatient with my spiritual growth? What about the spiritual growth of others I know? What can I say or do to communicate more grace to others in this area of my life? What areas of impatience do I need to admit and confess to the Lord? What areas of impatience do I need to admit and seek forgiveness from others.

Day #7 - He knows

And every branch that bears fruit He prunes. (John 15:2)

Attention to detail is an important mark of a good leader, but this does not mean he or she has to be intimately involved in every single decision. Instead, keeping the big picture firmly in mind, he or she coordinates the efforts of team members as they work through these items and report back their findings. As the leader helps them understand what direction the team is going, he or she can make good decisions based upon the vision, shared values and established objectives.

Although God is all-powerful and all-knowing.
He is fully aware of every detail of your life.

The vinedresser has complete and perfect knowledge of all things. He knows where he wants to lead us to. Our future is unknown to us, but the Lord knows what's far ahead and what's next for our lives. The vinedresser gently leads us as the Spirit of God takes the Word of God and moves our hearts to follow the will of God. This path often walks us through the valley of hardship, suffering, and loss. But there's no need to fear this valley. Why not? God himself walks with us and remains in us each step of the way.

Although God is all-powerful and all-knowing, He is intimately involved with every area of your life. Not only is God completely aware of your surroundings, He is also intimately involved with each and every step you take. The wisdom of the divine vinedresser allows Him to take care of His garden in a way that is beyond our capacity to understand or predict. God is fully aware of every detail of your life. David wrote,

O Lord, You have searched me and known me. You know my sitting down and my rising up; You understand my thought afar off. You comprehend my path and my lying down, and are acquainted with all my ways. For there is not a word on my tongue, but behold, O Lord, You know it altogether. (Psalm 139:1-4)

This level of involvement should lead us to an incredible confidence in our great Lord. God knows us intimately, he watches over us, and He is intentionally involved with every detail of our lives. No matter how difficult life gets, remember that he knows exactly what you are experiencing. The Lord knows your circumstances; He knows how things will affect your family; and He knows exactly what is needed to draw you closer to Him.

He knows us intimately, He watches over us, and He's
intentionally involved with every detail of our lives.

The vinedresser has everything under His control so don't worry for a minute. The psalmist masterfully wrote:

He counts the number of the stars; He calls them all by name. Great is our Lord, and mighty in power; His understanding is infinite. (Psalm 147:4-5)

No matter what happens to the other branches, no matter how hard it rains or how others try to destroy the vine, the Lord is in complete control. God knows what He is doing, so simply rest in Him. During those restless nights, rest your hope in the Lord, He's got you covered. He is fully aware of what is happening to you and understands the challenges. He has experienced the pain. He knows the numbers. He knows every detail.

God himself walks with us and remains in us each step of the way.

Receive: Recognize the Lord for His infinite wisdom and awesome power. Praise Him for who He is and what He has done. Continue studying and memorizing John 3:16 and Romans 3:23. Continue reading one chapter a day from the Gospel of John.

Rejoice: Open your Bible and read Matthew 6:30. Prayerfully consider the following: Is my faith so shallow or small that I can't trust Almighty God to handle the details of my life?

Release: What painful difficulties have I experienced recently? Have I responded by faith and obedience to God's Word or by complaining and turning to destructive habits? Who can I encourage today with what I learned as a result of this great difficulty?

Day # 8 - Growth through Discomfort

And every branch that bears fruit He prunes, that it may bear more fruit. (John 15:2)

Stretch marks are discouraging for teenagers. When the body grows faster than the skin can handle, these ugly marks can quickly appear without warning on the body. Certain creams can help remove the marks, but usually not fast enough. Some of these marks may remain visible for many years. Some marks may never fade completely.

In any delivery system, problems can be expected and marks can last longer than expected. Trucks run out of gas and get delayed in traffic. Severe weather increases time in transit and shuts down delivery routes. Delivery people sometimes deliver packages to the wrong address. These problems are not predictable, but expected as seasons change.

In God's delivery system, problems sometimes arise not because you're doing something wrong, but because you're doing something right. You might say, "That doesn't make any sense." If you understand the great metaphor of John 15, it makes perfect sense, because problems can lead you to a greater level of intimacy with the vine. Anything that leads us to greater relational intimacy with Christ is worth enduring.

> Problems can lead you to a greater
> level of intimacy with the vine.

When the branch begins to grow and produce fruit, it experiences new challenges. The branches start getting heavier and may shoot out in too many directions at once. Although this may sound good, it isn't at all. This additional weight has the potential to strain the branch. Excess greenery, beautiful though it is, can divert essential energy from the production of fruit. These factors can ultimately affect your connection back to the vine.

> When the branch begins to grow and produce fruit,
> it experiences new challenges.

We have limited time and energy. We only have twenty-four hours in a day. Our bodies need time to sleep and recover to maximize the time we spend awake during the day. When we give our precious time and energy to people or activities outside of God's plan for our lives, He often creates a sudden interruption to refocus us in the right direction. Why does He do this? The reason is rather simple. The vinedresser wants us to produce more fruit. With this goal in mind, He begins to cut out of our lives what distracts us from being more fruitful. He begins to prune our lives.

The vinedresser wants to produce an abundance of fruit through your life. For this reason, He will sometimes remove the excess from your life to keep you solidly connected to the vine and maximize your fruitfulness. This will require great discomfort on your part, but in the end, it will not compare to what He plans to do through your life. The vinedresser removes the excess from your life to strengthen your connection to the vine. Don't forget this key point. Your suffering has a divine purpose.

> The vinedresser removes the excess from your life
> to point you to the vine.

Spiritual growth often comes as we endure personal pain. Paul reminds us:

> Not only that, but we rejoice in our sufferings, knowing that suffering produces endurance, and endurance produces character, and character produces hope, and hope does not put us to shame, because God's love has been poured into our hearts through the Holy Spirit who has been given to us. (Romans 5:3-5)

Receive: Spend some time with the Father, asking Him to prepare you for the coming discomforts of your spiritual growth. Ask Him to help you draw closer to the vine during this process. Continue reading through the Gospel of John and review all of your memory verses out loud.

Rejoice: Open your Bible and read Philippians 4:14. Celebrate what God is teaching you through his Word?

Release: Am I encouraging others through their pain? Am I ready to grow through personal pain? As a result of these truths, what might need to change in my attitude, beliefs, and actions? Who can I share this with today?

Day # 9 - Growth through Pain

He prunes, that it may bear more fruit. (John 15:2)

Trimming hedges is never a one-time activity. In the rainy season, you may have to trim your hedges two to three times a month. If not, once a month may work well. Removing excess shrubbery takes considerable time and effort. It takes the right equipment and the right skillset to get the job done right. The one doing the work determines exactly what needs to be cut. He or she reduces the height, width and length of the hedges to produce a stronger hedge over the course of time.

At just the right time, the vinedresser steps into the vineyard of your life and clips away the excess shrubbery. He removes what is unnecessary and temporary from our lives to produce what brings Him glory. This pruning process may be more than simply uncomfortable; it can be very painful. God will remove the excess from your life to draw you closer to the vine. The excess may be a prized possession, a job, savings, some recurring event, a close friendship, or something else you really value.

At just the right time, the vinedresser steps into the vineyard of your life and clips away the excess shrubbery.

God has a purpose for everything He removes. He only removes what is absolutely necessary for you to produce more fruit. God allows you to experience pain to further expand his presence here on earth. Don't try to figure it all out. God may decide to reveal His purpose for your pain, or He may not. Sometimes the only explanation we can find for what God removes from our lives is the comfort we're able to bring to others who experience a similar loss. Yet, there is good news—you can trust the vinedresser. God cares for you deeply and he knows what He is doing.

God has a purpose for everything He removes.

When you experience trials, do you complain and criticize God's ways? Do you submit to God's Word regardless of your circumstances? Will you let God use the pain, discomfort and loss in your life for his eternal purposes and glory? If we allow Him, God can also use our difficulties to bring great comfort and encouragement to others. Paul wrote:

Blessed be the God and Father of our Lord Jesus Christ, the Father of mercies and God of all comfort, who comforts us in all our tribulation, that we may be able to comfort those who are in any trouble, with the comfort with which we ourselves are comforted by God. (2 Corinthians 1:3-4)

Although it can be extremely painful, difficult experiences can lead you to a greater level of fruitfulness. The less you have to weigh you down, the more fruit your life can deliver for the vinedresser. Don't allow yourself to get discouraged by the pruning process. Removing the excess is never pleasant for the branch. Be grateful to the Lord for His infinite wisdom, and rest fully in the fact that He has a purpose for everything He removes.

Consider the following questions prayerfully as you reflect on what the vinedresser may be planning to remove in the near future:

- Do I have a job or business which overwhelmingly consumes my time, energy, and focus?
- Does it serve as a constant source of conflict within my family?
- Do I maintain friendships which influence me to sin against God?
- Do my possessions continue to demand more of my time, energy, and finances?
- What areas of my life are doing better today than ever before?
- What personal hobbies serve no eternal purpose?
- What forms of entertainment plant unholy thoughts in my mind?
- What areas of responsibility am I managing well?
- What areas of responsibility am I neglecting?
- In what areas of my life is God clearly blessing?
- Am I depending more on people rather than on the Lord to provide for my needs?

Receive: Open your Bible and read John 15:1-11. Ask God to prepare your heart for the excess that needs to be removed from your life. Make it a point to trust Him during this process and draw closer to the vine. Begin memorizing 1 Peter 3:18 and review the previous memory verses.

Rejoice: Prayerfully consider the following: Do I trust God to remove what he desires from my life to produce more fruit and bring glory to his name?

Release: What relationships, areas of success, or opportunities has the Lord recently "clipped away" and removed from my life? How has the Lord used this experience to draw me closer to him?

Day # 10 - Connected Securely

You are already clean because of the word which I have spoken to you. (John 15:3)

When you get ready to ride a fast rollercoaster, you want to make sure your body is as secure as possible. The reason for this is simple; not taking the necessary precautions can lead to serious injury or even death. Since you value your life, taking these extra measures is no problem at all. You won't be bothered by unexpected delays if it means making you safer.

Your connection to the vine is totally secure.

At the moment of your salvation, your sins were forgiven and cleansed. Although you were separated from God due to your sin, Jesus died to connect you to God and make things right. You were grafted into the vine, Jesus Christ, by the power of the Holy Spirit. Your attachment to the vine is now totally secure. The very one who connected you guarantees this eternal connection. Paul wrote to the Ephesian believers:

In Him you also trusted, after you heard the word of truth, the gospel of your salvation; in whom also, having believed, you were sealed with the Holy Spirit of promise, who is the guarantee of our inheritance until the redemption of the purchased possession, to the praise of His glory. (Ephesians 1:13-14)

The vinedresser initiated your connection to the vine. You did not initiate a spiritual relationship with Jesus. This is a work of God's Spirit. God is the initiator and sustainer of your salvation. The Lord secures our relationship forever; we do not. The Lord guarantees our eternal salvation by grace through faith in Christ; we do not. The Lord seals us through the Holy Spirit as a guarantee of our salvation; we do not. Jesus said:

My sheep hear My voice, and I know them, and they follow Me. And I give them eternal life, and they shall never perish; neither shall anyone snatch them out of My hand. My Father, who has given them to Me, is greater than all; and no one is able to snatch them out of My Father's hand. (John 10:27-30)

Your connection to the vine was initiated by the vinedresser.

What does all this security really mean? It means that you can rest fully in the work of the vinedresser. You can rest in the absolute certainty of His promises. You can trust His provision, protection, and eternal guarantee for your life. It means that you can focus more on the vine and completely eliminate any worry or fear from your thinking.

The Apostle Paul wrote:

> For I am persuaded that neither death nor life, nor angels nor principalities nor powers, nor things present nor things to come, nor height nor depth, nor any other created thing, shall be able to separate us from the love of God which is in Christ Jesus our Lord. (Romans 8:38-39)

You are completely secure as a result of the finished work of Jesus Christ on the cross at Calvary. It is finished! Your eternal life is secure in Christ Jesus. If death is approaching, don't panic. Jesus overcame death. Death no longer has power over your life. Death is simply a door into the next phase of your eternity. It is a transition to the eternal promises which await us in Christ Jesus our Lord. You are eternally secure in Christ.

The Spirit of God has washed away our sins. We are clean and forever holy in God's sight. The blood of Jesus Christ has cleansed us from all of our sins. As God's holy temple, we stand as living stones, holy children of the Living God. We have been justified by faith and made right with God. We now have eternal peace with God through our Lord Jesus Christ. We are already clean; we have been lifted up through Christ.

Receive: Ask the Lord in your time of prayer today to help you learn how to trust Him more. Keep reading through the Gospel of John and memorizing 1 Peter 3:18.

Rejoice: Prayerfully consider the following: Since I have eternal life right now in the Lord Jesus Christ, do I really need to fear dying?

Release: What part of my relationship with the Lord is strong and secure? What part of my relationship with the Lord do I still have questions or uncertainties about? How can I encourage others today to remain strong in the Lord and fully trust God's Word?

Abiding Thoughts

Remembering is critical to my spiritual well-being.

Listening is first of all a spiritual disciplines, because faith comes by hearing and hearing by the word of God. Listening is receiving.

A blessed person is one who is like a little child who can only live by receiving from a source of continuous love.

To be perfect is to live with a heart completely open to God and a heart completely open to man.

Living now with an open heart is true spirituality.

Now is what God is allowing to reveal the true state of my heart. My open heart right now is my witness and my opportunity to glorify God.

Glorifying God is to reveal His open heart. His heart never closes.

Seeking my happiness is to seek God. Seeking my happiness must be my first priority in life.

The pursuit of happiness is not evil. To want to feel good is to want to feel God.

Day # 11 - A Continuous Surrender

Abide in Me, and I in you. (John 15:4)

The gasoline station has one primary purpose: to refill your car with fuel to get you back on your journey. Your car will eventually burn all of this new gasoline and require more fuel for the ride. Every mile you drive brings you one mile closer to the next time you need to refill your vehicle. In the same way, as believers in Christ, we need to stop and refuel spiritually every day. This is essential to our personal health and fruitfulness.

To be refilled with God's Spirit and empowered for the Lord's service is critical for our effectiveness in the Christian life. We are not the ones doing the filling; God refills us. Our job is to position ourselves to be good receivers. Are you a grateful receiver? Are you asking the Lord daily to fill you with his Spirit and to empower you to serve others in love? For effectiveness to increase, our continuous surrender to God's will must also increase. This increase is in both in quality and in frequency.

Your connection to the vine is a growing, life-giving relationship. Your most important role as a branch is to continually remain in the vine and allow the vine to freely live in you. Jesus, through the power of the Holy Spirit, is the one producing spiritual fruit. For what purpose? The purpose is to glorify God and bless others. But don't forget; we are not the producers. If we are willing, we serve as recipients and conduits of God's love towards others. We serve as a channel of God's immeasurable blessings to a lost and broken world.

Remember, you can trust the vinedresser as He carries out His plan through the vine. Your continuous surrender to the desires of the vinedresser makes it possible for the vine to freely live through you. Surrendering to Christ actually represents your freedom in Christ.

> Your most important role as a branch is to continually remain in the vine and allow the vine to freely live in you.

Satan, the enemy, will aggressively oppose your spiritual surrender. He will use fear, doubt, and temptation to shift your thinking from surrender to dissatisfaction. He loves to deceive God's people by removing their focus from the vine. Satan wants you to seek satisfaction somewhere else. Here's the bottom line of all this opposition and distraction—Satan wants to destroy you (Genesis 3:1-5). Be alert! This is his ultimate goal.

> Satan wants you to find satisfaction somewhere else.

For this reason, the process of spiritual surrender is a daily, moment-by-moment activity, not simply a one-time event. To experience the abiding life, let Jesus refill you continuously as you surrender continuously and submit unreservedly to God's will and purposes for your life.

The apostle Paul develops this idea with regards to our relationship with the Holy Spirit in his letters. He gives us a very powerful command as he encourages believers to live wisely. Paul wants us to stop searching for external satisfaction, to stop being consumed by worldly living and temporary pleasures. He wants us to be constantly filled with God's Spirit. His command is both clear and direct:

Be filled with the Spirit. (Ephesians 5:18)

God wants you to be constantly filled with His Spirit. He wants you to get rid of your old way of living and allow his Son to guide your every thought, word, and action. When you allow God to replace the satisfaction you once found in the world with the life-giving satisfaction found in his Son, He can bring your life great freedom and contentment as you discover your new purpose for living. Don't just live your life. Refill your spirit by continuously surrendering to the will of God as revealed in the Son of God.

Receive: Open your Bible and read 1 Peter 4:6.

Rejoice: Prayerfully consider the following: Am I living in the Spirit? Am I daily going before the Lord to change me and fill me with his Spirit?

Release: What has been the most valuable to me regarding taking the time to receive from Christ each day and remain in His presence? What sins and fears has the Lord helped me overcome? What friends, family members, neighbors or co-workers can I share this with today?

Day # 12 - Spiritual Productivity

Abide in Me, and I in you. As the branch cannot bear fruit of itself, unless it abides in the vine, neither can you, unless you abide in Me. (John 15:4)

Our culture loves to measure productivity. We use charts, graphs, and many other tools to help us quantify performance, profitability, and assess efficiency. Measuring an employee's speed, efficiency, and quality of work is normal. It helps us establish standards for performance and forecast costs and profits. But in the spiritual world, spiritual productivity is measured very differently. It is a measurement of an abiding life in Christ.

Think about the amount of time you spend in prayer before taking action. What does your commitment to prayer say about your dependence on the Lord? Total dependence on the vine always precedes spiritual productivity. A continuous surrender to the will of the vinedresser will naturally lead you to depend on Him fully, both for spiritual productivity and growth. A life characterized by continuous surrender and total dependence on the vine is the work of the vinedresser; then and only then can His work through your life thrive greatly.

Spiritual productivity is relational, not mechanical. This is so difficult for many of us to understand and practice. We want to follow proven steps, short formulas, and innovative models to produce spiritual fruit. But at the heart of spiritual productivity is a genuine relationship with the Savior. There are no shortcuts, no magical formulas, and no clever models to follow. As we carve out time to remain in the presence of the Lord, we learn to grow deeper in our walk with Christ. And this rich spiritual experience is contagious. Our soul is refreshed. We then begin to increase our time with the Lord and encourage others to do the same.

Total dependence on the vine precedes spiritual productivity.

Everyone has limitations. As a branch, you must recognize your spiritual limitations. You can't produce the visible fruit of God's Spirit without being regularly connected to the vine. The focus of the Christian life is primarily connectivity to the vine rather than activity for the vine. Your connectivity in Christ is what determines your activity for Christ. There is a direct relationship between dependence and fruit: as your dependence on the vine increases, the visible fruit of God's Spirit working through your life will increase as well. Don't focus on the fruit. Focus on growing your relationship in Christ as you remain continuously connected the the vine.

The focus of the Christian life is connectivity
to the vine rather than activity for the vine.

Your connectivity is what determines your activity.

Focus your full attention on the vine. Ask God to increase your capacity to depend fully on Him. Total dependence involves resting securely in the vine and trusting in the complete care of the vinedresser. You are not required to manufacture a product, an experience, or an event. The vine, Jesus Christ, now lives within you. He is responsible for the results; you are responsible for abiding and following what He leads you to do.

The vine produces everything needed to produce God's visible presence on earth. God's fruit through your life is produced from the inside out, and there is a direct relationship between dependence and fruit. Prayerfully dedicate your complete dependence on Jesus. Submit your will to God's will. Replace your plans with God's plans. Ask the Lord to help you trust His word as He directs your life each day.

Incline your ear, O Lord, and answer me, for I am poor and needy. Preserve my life, for I am godly; save your servant, who trusts in you—you are my God. (Psalm 86:1-3)

There is a direct relationship between dependence and fruit.

Receive: Open your Bible and read all of Psalm 86.

Rejoice: Prayerfully consider the following: Am I depending on God as if He were my only hope? What new things have I learned about His ways?

Release: What needs to change in my attitude, beliefs, and actions? What steps do I need to take outwardly? What friends, family members, neighbors or co-workers can I share this with today?

Day # 13 - Complete Provision

I am the vine, you are the branches. (John 15:5)

Throughout history, there are many examples of great people who have crossed cultural, economic, and ethnic barriers to provide for the needs of others. These heroes do not always appear on the covers of national magazines, but their good works and their generosity are never forgotten. They are often motivated by love, strong convictions, and the future well-being of others. These providers are often characterized as selfless, giving, tenacious, and resilient. Who would you say is your provider?

Everything you need to live the Christian life is sourced and provided through the vine. The Lord is our Provider. He is the one who takes care of us. There is no need to worry, fear, or lose sleep. God knows exactly what you need and when you need it. You can trust completely in God's provision for your daily needs and let His word radically transform your old way of thinking. Before you can rest you have to trust. Before we can truly rest in the Lord, we have to trust in His ability to provide for our needs:

Be anxious for nothing, but in everything by prayer and supplication, with thanksgiving, let your requests be made known to God; and the peace of God, which surpasses all understanding, will guard your hearts and minds through Christ Jesus. Finally, brethren, whatever things are true, whatever things are noble, whatever things are just, whatever things are pure, whatever things are lovely, whatever things are of good report, if there is any virtue and if there is anything praiseworthy—meditate on these things. (Philippians 4:6-8)

Everything you need to live the Christian life
is sourced and provided through the vine.

Waiting for the provision of the vinedresser is another component of total dependence. We don't necessarily adjust automatically to this new reality in Christ. God's ways are not our ways and His methods of providing for our needs often move us far beyond our comfort zone. You may need to undo old life management techniques and begin new ones. When problems arise, strengthen your connection to the vine. Make asking and receiving from God your first priority, not your last resort. God wants to be first in our lives not second or last. Be wise as you walk on your journey of faith and remember the wise counsel from the Book of Proverbs:

Trust in the Lord with all your heart and lean not on your own understanding;
in all your ways acknowledge Him and He shall direct your paths. (Proverbs 3:5-6)

Replace worry, fear, and manipulation with trust, faith, and truthfulness. The vinedresser may occasionally shake your branch, but hold on for the ride. Remember who you're connected to—Jesus. Don't try to solve your problems without Him. Immediately invite the Lord to take full control of every situation and direct your steps right from the start. Trust Him, and you will be glad you did! Make a list of the things He has provided for you during this last month. You might be pleasantly surprised with the results.

Receive: Open your Bible and read 1 Timothy 6:17.

Rejoice: Prayerfully consider the following: How have I seen God provide richly for my family? List some examples below from this last month:

Have I expressed gratitude to Him recently? What am I most grateful for?

Release: Do I trust the Lord as my Provider? As I look at my decisions and attitudes related to education, career, finances, and others, do they reflect a life of total dependence on the Lord? What should I start changing as a result of my lack of trust in one or more of these areas?

Day # 14 - Total Replacement

I have been crucified with Christ; it is no longer I who live, but Christ lives in me; and the life which I now live in the flesh I live by faith in the Son of God, who loved me and gave Himself for me. (Galatians 2:20)

Replacing things that break is not something most people look forward to. It is usually done out of pure obligation. It can be uncomfortable and very costly, sometimes taking more effort than what you planned for. But the new item is often more superior to what it replaces! It often is built with more innovative machinery and higher quality materials. What you are now getting is more resilient. This is even truer in the spiritual realm, when our lives are permanently replaced by the eternal life of Jesus Christ.

Although you're the one breathing, you're no longer the one living. Jesus is the One living through your life.

Your spiritual transformation took place immediately at the moment of your salvation. Your old nature has been put to death and fully replaced with God's holy nature. In Christ, you are God's holy temple. Although you are the one breathing, you are no longer the one living. Jesus is the One living through your life. The more you let His life flow through you, the more productive you will be as a branch in connecting others to the vine. Remember, you've been changed; your old nature has been replaced.

Your purpose for living has been radically changed. God's Word defines your new purpose. You are now a son or a daughter of the King of Glory. You no longer live in the past or need to seek satisfaction from ungodly desires. Your past behavior no longer defines who you are. In Christ, you have a new spiritual eternity. It is sealed and guaranteed by the Holy Spirit. Your purpose and satisfaction for living have been completely replaced. You now live by faith and not by sight.

The more you let His life flow through you, the more productive you will be in connecting others to the vine.

The "old you" died and was buried; it has been replaced forever. You are free to discover God's unfolding purpose for your life by faith, as you abide in the vine and respond in obedience to His word. Although your spiritual transformation was instantaneous, the life-application of your conversion is a steady process. You grow by the grace of God as you remain connected to the vine and allow God's Word to change you from within. Are you living from the overflow of your new nature?

Your purpose for living has been radically changed.

As you read through the Gospel of John, take time to pray, memorize scripture, and study each devotional carefully. The quality of your devotional life directly impacts your effectiveness as a branch. We produce fruit out of the overflow of our relationship with Christ. Fruit is not produced as a result of an abundance of activities. Receive well and listen carefully to what the Lord leads you to follow and practice. Ask yourself, "How does my life need to change in light of this truth?" The answer is the life-application that you need to put into practice. Live by faith in Christ as you learn to apply God's Word in your life every day.

Remember the words of the Apostle Paul:

All Scripture is breathed out by God and profitable for teaching, for reproof, for correction, and for training in righteousness, that the man of God may be complete, equipped for every good work. (2 Timothy 3:16-17)

Although your spiritual transformation was instantaneous, the life-application of your conversion is a steady process.

Receive: Open your Bible and read Romans 6:6.

Rejoice: Prayerfully consider the following: Since my old life has been replaced in Christ Jesus, what is my next step to grow spiritually?

Release: Do I have one or more areas of my life where God is off limits? Is there an attitude or behavior needing replacement and transformation? As a result of these truths, what might need to change in my attitude, beliefs, and actions?

Day # 15 - Simplify: Less for More

I am the vine, you are the branches. He who abides in Me, and I in him, bears much fruit; for without Me you can do nothing. (John 15:5)

One characteristic of a genius is their ability to take a complex problem, break it down into stages, and deliver a practical solution to make it work. For the rest of us, life's problems are not always so easy to understand, interpret, and correct. At times our desire to solve difficult problems brings out additional challenges in the process for us to decipher. But there's good news! Life in the Spirit is simple, not complicated.

The most natural and productive activity for a branch is to abide in the vine. Without the vine, the branch cannot live, grow, or produce fruit. The branch depends exclusively on the vine for ongoing nourishment and so should we. By itself, the branch can do NOTHING. You cannot fulfill your purpose without remaining in the vine. Be still. Stop adding things to your calendar to keep busy. You don't need more events, activities, and responsibilities to grow; you actually need less. Remember, you were redeemed to remain in the presence of Jesus Christ.

> The most natural and productive activity
> for a branch is to abide in the vine.

You must allow the vinedresser to remove all unnecessary attitudes, activities, and distractions to focus greater attention on the vine. You can't fulfill your purpose as a believer unless you receive from the vine and allow Christ's life to regularly live and flow through your life.

> You can't fulfill your purpose as a believer unless you receive
> from the vine and allow His life to live through you.

As a branch, the energy and focus of your life must be radically simplified; receive, rejoice, and release. The more you simplify your daily relationship with Christ, the greater the potential to produce much fruit. Your life as a believer can make a huge difference when you do what you were created to do. You were redeemed to remain. And as you remain in Christ, you will be well. As a branch, your "doing" is not about filling your schedule with more activities, events, and commitments. On the contrary, your "doing" involves reducing. In the Christian life, when you reduce you produce. When you don't reduce you can't produce.

> The more you simplify your daily relationship with Christ,
> the greater the potential to produce much fruit.

The more you simplify your daily relationship with Christ, the greater the potential to produce more fruit becomes a reality. Here is the simplicity of the Christian life: your daily satisfaction and spiritual productivity is found in Jesus Christ. You were saved to experience complete satisfaction and daily spiritual nourishment in the vine. This is "the main thing." This is at the heart of an abiding relationship with Christ. And in the Christian life, when you reduce you produce. In the spiritual world, less is actually more. God wants your relationship with him to thrive. The Apostle Paul wrote:

> Not that we are sufficient in ourselves to claim anything as coming from us, but our sufficiency is from God. (2 Corinthians 3:5)

Abiding is the only way to be of any use to God. What do you need to reduce in your life to focus more carefully on the vine? Take steps today to start reducing these activities.

In the Christian life, when you reduce you produce.

Receive: Open your Bible and read John 15:1-11.

Rejoice: Prayerfully consider the following: What is the main thing I need to stop or adjust in my life to spend more time with the Lord Jesus?

Release: What activities or habits have increasingly demanded more and more of my energy and time? What more important areas have suffered as a result of this shift? How is the Lord leading me to make adjustments in these areas?

Abiding Thoughts

Abiding is the only way to be of any use to God.

Fruit that remains is the satisfaction that comes to me from God
and now remains in someone else as well.

The health of a church is determined by the level of
satisfaction being found in God.

No church can move faster than the speed of its satisfaction in God.

Essence must precede effort in church life.
Essence is determined by what we receive, not what we do.

Confession of sin is needed so I can locate the place
where I became an outcome controller instead of a loving decider.

Confession of sin is needed so I can find the place
where my heart closes to God and to others.

I sin less only because I abide more.

Day # 16 - The True Vine

If anyone does not abide in Me, he is cast out as a branch and is withered; and they gather them and throw them into the fire, and they are burned. (John 15:6)

It looks identical to the one in the department store, but the price is 75% less. You pick up the item and examine it very carefully. It looks just like the real thing. What a great deal! Or it would be, if it weren't a fake. Today we find fake jewelry, fake news, fake data, and other deceptions. There are many counterfeits in the world. For this reason, it really does pay to check things out. This is why we often have to investigate declarations and claims before we can discover their true validity and identity.

Jesus is the Living Vine, the One who is Life
and delivers life to those who trust in Him.

There are many vines in the world of spiritual vineyards, but only one True Vine under the care of the master vinedresser. Jesus was actively involved in creation (John 1). He is the Beginning and the End, the Alpha and the Omega. Jesus is Eternal. He is the only True Vine, and God's only solution to your sin problem. Jesus is real life!

Jesus' life produces life.

Jesus is the Living Vine, the One who is the Life and delivers life to those who trust in Him. The crucified and risen Christ is God's only provision to completely satisfy the payment and penalty for your sins. Jesus is the True Vine; there is no other. All those who reject Him will face eternal separation from God. The Apostle Peter told the religious leaders:

This [Jesus] is the 'stone which was rejected by you builders, which has become the chief cornerstone.' Nor is there salvation in any other, for there is no other name under heaven given among men by which we must be saved. (Acts 4:11-12)

Jesus died on the cross to connect you to God. He was buried, and on the third day, rose from the grave. Mohammed, Buddha, Confucius, and others have all died. Each one of them remains buried in the grave. Their teachings may have continued, but they did not produce eternal fruit nor connect others with the Father. These men were not the True Vine. They could not restore their own lives or produce new life for others.

Jesus' life produced life. You can't produce life if you are not the Life. Jesus is the Life and therefore, only He can produce Life in you. Moreover, Jesus produces life in everyone who believes in Him and turns from their sins. What an amazing Savior we have. The life of Christ dwells in us. Jesus is sufficient for whatever we face. In Christ, we find our life; in Christ, we find our hope; in Christ, we find rest for our souls.

> Jesus said to him, "I am the way, the truth, and the life.
> No one comes to the Father except through Me. (John 14:6)

Make a list of people you know that have not followed Jesus as Savior. Make it a point this week to pray for them by name and share these truths with them. Jesus is the hope of the world and the True Vine. Jesus gives life to everyone who calls on His name as they believe in the message of the gospel and repent from their sins.

Receive: Open your Bible and read Isaiah 42:6.

Rejoice: Prayerfully consider the following: How can I creatively and effectively share with others this week the hope and promises of Jesus?

Release: What friends, family members, neighbors or co-workers can I share this with today?

Day # 17 - A Productive Conversation

If you abide in Me, and My words abide in you, you will ask
what you desire, and it shall be done for you. (John 15:7)

In general, there is a sharp distinction between the general length of conversations of boys and girls. Typically girls love to talk and boys prefer action over conversation. Girls are highly relational and personal in their interactions. Boys tend to be rough, less verbal, but very competitive. Bridging this social gap as they develop through life is quite a challenge.

Your prayers are spiritually productive
when they are aligned with God's word.

You may enjoy talking very much or very little. But did you know that Prayer is simply talking with God in the form of a conversation. Prayer has been described as the spiritual oxygen of the Christian life. There is a direct relationship between prayer and abiding. Prayer can bring you closer to God by helping you grow deeper in your daily fellowship and dependence on the vine. As you sharpen your focus on the things that matter most to God, the Lord will guide you to pray in a way that magnifies His name by matching your desires with His desires.

As a branch, you want to be productive in the way you invest your time. Your prayers are spiritually productive when they are aligned with God's Word. As you memorize God's Word and reflect on it throughout your day, something changes: you. The Word begins to change the way you think, process, and respond to your environment. This is a good change. God's Word keeps you on the right track. The Apostle Paul wrote:

All Scripture is given by inspiration of God, and is profitable for doctrine, for reproof, for correction, for instruction in righteousness, that the man of God may be complete, thoroughly equipped for every good work. (2 Timothy 3:16-17)

A regular study of God's Word and an open conversation about how it applies to every area of your life will lead you to productive spiritual conversations. When God's Word fills and directs your life, the vinedresser will respond to your prayers. The Lord not only wants to hear our words of praise, thanksgiving, and repentance, He wants to hear us ask Him for the things which align with His heart. He wants us to talk with Him about those who are taken advantage of, the neglected, those struggling with sin, people who need salvation, the poor, the widows, the orphans, those without a place to call home, those in hospitals and in prisons and those who are sick. Ask God for the things which matter to him.

The Word of God begins to change the way you think, process, and respond to your environment.

Prayer and personal application of God's Word should work together. Ask the Lord to search your heart for anything out of alignment with His Word. Confess it right away, and thank the Lord for His great mercy and compassion. When you abide in Jesus Christ, God's Word abides in you. As you pray according to God's Word and in alignment with His will, God responds. God is waiting for your next conversation. Make it a good one.

Abide in Jesus   God's Word Abides in You   Prayer   God Responds

Receive: Open your Bible and read Matthew 6:9.

Rejoice: Prayerfully consider the following: Since God is your Father, what kind of conversations do you think He is waiting for you to begin?

What do I need to stop asking for that I know is not a part of God's Word?

What have you always wanted to ask God for which aligns well with God's Word? Write it down and ask!

Release: As a result of these truths, what might need to change in my attitude, beliefs, and actions? Who can I share these truths with today?

Day # 18 - The Goal

By this My Father is glorified, that you bear much fruit. (John 15:8)

Every good team knows the importance of listening to their coach. They want to please their coach and respond well to his instructions. It helps when the coach can communicate his plan with as few words as possible. A clear understanding of the game plan helps the team remember their mission and pull together under great competition. The goal of clear communication is to simplify "the win" for each player.

The goal of bearing much fruit is simply to give God greater glory through His work in your life.

An Abiding Life	Bears Much Fruit	God is Glorified

The goal of the branch is to produce an abundance of fruit to praise the name of the vinedresser. God wants to produce a generous amount of fruit through your life to magnify His name for all eternity. This is "the win" for the Christian. The goal of bearing much fruit is simply to give God greater glory through His work in your life. Keep this in mind: the greater the fruit the greater the glory. The goal is to bring God greater glory. This is His plan for your life. This is an incredible privilege and responsibility.

Your life was designed to glorify God!

An abiding life is one which receives a regular flow of spiritual nourishment from the vine, and intentionally delivers this life to others to bear much fruit. When you allow God to freely produce much fruit through your life, His name is glorified and made known to others. God wants your life to generously magnify His name. God wants his fame to spread through His people. He wants you to be intentional about this.

God grafted you into His vineyard so your life would produce much fruit and glorify His name. Your life was designed to glorify God! In his infinite wisdom, God created you as His unique tool to make His light visible to others. Your gifts of speaking and serving others were specifically given to you to bring glory to God's name. Use what God has given you to deliver His love to others. You are an instrument for God's purposes. Use your gifts, leverage your skills, share your experiences, integrate your education, and maximize every talent and resource to glorify God's mighty name.

God wants your life to generously magnify His name.

Imagine the passion in the Apostle Peter's heart as he writes this note to the early church family:

As each one has received a gift, minister it to one another, as good stewards of the manifold grace of God. If anyone speaks, let him speak as the oracles of God. If anyone ministers, let him do it as with the ability which God supplies, that in all things God may be glorified through Jesus Christ, to whom belong the glory and the dominion forever and ever. Amen. (1 Peter 4:10-11)

Reflect on how you can use your skills, talents, experiences, education, training, along with your speaking and ministry gifts to magnify God's name to others this week. The goal is to bear the fruit of God's character through your life. God is counting on you to magnify His name. He's counting on you to be a channel of His love and grace to those around you. So don't wait another minute…get started.

Receive: Open your Bible and read Matthew 28:18-20.

Rejoice: Prayerfully consider the following: Since making disciples is part of bearing much fruit, whom will you begin to develop in their faith?

Release: Am I committed to glorifying God with my life? Am I trying to make my name great or God's name great? What can I start doing practically to make God's name known to more people?

Day # 19 - Clear Evidence

By this My Father is glorified, that you bear much fruit;
so you will be My disciples. (John 15:8)

Fruit is what you expect to find a few years after planting good seed in your garden. In time, you should expect a generous crop, not just enough to replace your original seed. In the world of agriculture, you reap more than what you sow. Planting good seed always carries the potential for generous multiplication. This is the natural product of good water, rich soil, careful pruning, and great care. More fruit is wonderful indeed.

Fruit is the evidence of a transformed life.

Your spiritual transformation is made evident by the fruit you deliver to others. A person who claims to be a Christian, but does not produce fruit, not even a small portion, is not a Christian. Fruit is the evidence of a transformed life and it should characterize your life as a believer. Fruit is the product of the Holy Spirit transforming us into the image of Christ. Fruit is evidence that you are rightly connected to the vine. As a branch, you should demonstrate the qualities which are characteristic of the vine.

Fruit is evidence that you are rightly connected to the vine.

These qualities of spiritual maturity are not developed all at once. It takes time to grow and produce fruit. You are an unfolding work of God. The vinedresser is more concerned with your consistency than with your speed. The goal of your transformation is the likeness of Jesus, being conformed into His very image. You have been transformed to be conformed into the image of Jesus Christ. Today, let the vinedresser perform his good and perfect work in your life. The Apostle Paul wrote:

And we know that all things work together for good to those who love God, to those who are the called according to His purpose. For whom He foreknew, He also predestined to be conformed to the image of His Son. (Romans 8:28 - 29)

As a wise vinedresser, God begins to remove those areas of your life which are in direct opposition to His divine plan. He also begins to develop you through a variety of experiences, leading you to manifest the attributes of the vine to get through each one. Some seasons of life will be difficult to endure, and others pleasantly sunny or cool. Rest assured, each of these is designed for your spiritual transformation and growth. The Lord never wastes an experience or a great personal difficulty in our lives. Each one can produce more fruit and magnify God's name.

You were transformed to be conformed
into the image of Jesus Christ.

As the Lord's branch, how is the life of Jesus being reflected through your attitude and through your actions? What is He asking you to change? Is there a new way for you to produce more fruit that you have yet to consider? These are great questions for personal reflection and prayer. Hopefully, what God wants to do through your life is becoming much clearer. Now you can see where the Lord wants to take us and how He wants to use our lives to love and serve others.

The vinedresser is more concerned with your consistency
than with your speed.

Receive: Open your Bible and read Romans 8:28-29.

Rejoice: Prayerfully consider the following: Is there a difficulty in my life right now that God wants to use to produce more spiritual fruit?

Release: Think about the habits in your life today and the patterns of thinking established over this last year. Understanding the simplicity of God's purpose for your life, what adjustments has the Lord been leading you to practice as a result of meditating on your purpose as a branch? Write down a few thoughts below.

Day # 20 - The Same Love

As the Father loved Me, I also have loved you; abide in My love. (John 15:9)

The love of a father has proven to be very powerful and transformational. Among other known positive contributions, the love of a father infuses tremendous confidence, unshakable stability, and peaceful security into the life of their children. These are only a few of the many benefits. There is a deep longing in our culture for strong, yet loving fathers to take their rightful place at home and within their communities.

With God, delivering love is very personal. Before the Lord inspired His people to write about the characteristics of love, He decided to first demonstrate His love and model what love is supposed to look like. As the vinedresser, God is the author and the initiator of true love. God took the first step by sending His only Son to die on the cross for your sins. He did this to connect you with the only source of life-giving satisfaction (John 3:16).

With God, delivering love is personal...very personal.

Make no mistake: the love of the Father regarding the Son is powerful, perfect, and eternal. Likewise, the love that Jesus has for you is powerful, perfect, and eternal. Remember, God wants us to live our Christian life in a growing relationship with Jesus. Our salvation was not the end, it was only the beginning of a lifelong spiritual fellowship with the Father through the Son. The Lord Jesus modeled this intimate relationship with the Father. The Father, Son, and Spirit have always existed in spiritual fellowship. Notice what John wrote about the Father and the Son, "the Word":

In the beginning was the Word, and the Word was with God, and the Word was God. He was in the beginning with God. All things were made through Him, and without Him nothing was made that was made. In Him was life, and the life was the light of men. (John 1:1-4)

The communication between Father, Son, and Spirit has always been clear and uninterrupted. They have shared complete knowledge, perfect unity, and infinite wisdom in every discussion. Jesus wants you to live in this very same love; a love that is unlimited in power, knowledge, wisdom, and unity. He wants you to receive this love from Him every moment of every day, and deliver this powerful, life-changing love to others. The love that Jesus has for you is great, perfect, and eternal. This love is not common; it is unique and uncommon. This amazing love is supernatural.

The love that Jesus has for you is great, perfect, and eternal.

The world today needs to see this same love. They need to see how Jesus would respond in a given situation. People need to see the beauty of God's perfect presence unfolded through the lives of his people. People today need to see a love that goes far beyond culture and political correctness. People need to see a love that gives generously instead of takes, one that sacrifices instead of demands and serves willingly rather than burdens others. Such a love can only be divine.

> People need to see the beauty of God's perfect presence unfolded through the lives of His people.

Receive: Open your Bible and read 1 John 4:18.

Rejoice: Prayerfully consider the following: Am I loving others "as the Father loved" me? Am I holding back love for others because of my personal fears or insecurities? If so, why?

Release: What stops me from loving others more? What holds me back from loving people without expecting anything in return? What fears restrict my love from flowing to others?

Abiding Thoughts

Complexity is of the devil. Simplicity is of God.

When I cooperate with God's intentions I feel like a man who just ate
a wonderful meal for free.

Spiritual habits are life disciplines that put me in the best position to receive
all Jesus is constantly willing to give to me.

The Sermon on the Mount is a description of the kind of life that will emerge
when I am perfectly satisfied in God 24 hours a day and seven days a week.

To believe is to receive.

To increase my faith means to increase my capacity to receive
what God has done, is doing or will do.

The Kingdom of God is a place where every heart remains
continuously open to God and everyone else.

To pray in Jesus' name is to pray in harmony with His intentions.

Every church can be perfectly healthy.

I am always obsessing on something or someone.
When I obsess on Jesus the best me emerges naturally.

Day # 21 - An Obedient Love

If you keep My commandments, you will abide in My love,
just as I have kept My Father's commandments and abide in His love. (John 15:10)

No matter how great one's dreams and hopes may be to build a home, unless someone draws up the blueprints, nothing happens. The dream will never become a reality and hope will fade until action is taken. Action is what makes the dream become a reality. This reminds us of an important principle: when love is present, action follows. In the spiritual world, love is perfected by obedience—taking action according to God's Word.

Your love for God is perfected through
your obedience to His word.

Love and obedience are two sides of the same coin. Your love for God is demonstrated by, and perfected through, your obedience to God's Word. Jesus modeled the beauty of perfect love through His unwavering obedience to the Father's commandments. Jesus obeyed God's Word 100% of the time. The Lord Jesus did not compromise, neglect, or delay His obedience. He followed God wholeheartedly in total obedience.

When you don't obey you can't abide. Obedience is the gateway to living an abiding life. Moreover, obedience is the door to spiritual life and fruitfulness. There's no such thing as a disobedient abiding believer. This is a spiritual contradiction. When you abide you obey and when you obey you abide. Love is perfected through obedience. Are you consistently obedient to what you learn about God's Word? If not, why not?

Obedience is the gateway to living an abiding life.

Perfecting your love for God is simple, not complex. The famous slogan from Nike, "Just do it," reminds people to put on the right equipment and take immediate action. Likewise, as you learn something new from God's Word, make it a habit to take immediate action. Practice what you learn right away. Never put off for tomorrow what God shows you to do today.

Following God's Word is never dull. It is an exhilarating adventure! Don't neglect or overanalyze your obedience to God's Word. This will paralyze your spiritual maturity and create patterns of sinful attitudes and behaviors in your life. Just do it! Remember, your obedience is the gateway to living an abiding life. Obedience is the key which unlocks spiritual vitality, fruitfulness, and immeasurable joy in Christ Jesus.

*As you learn something new from God's word,
make it a habit to take immediate action and "just do it."*

Whether the subject is prayer, giving, forgiveness, baptism, or something else, "just do it" and trust the vinedresser to work out the rest. He is worthy of your praise and worthy of your deepest confidence. As you practice God's Word, your intimacy with the vine will grow deeper. Allow God's unfailing love to grow and be perfected in you as you take the next step of faith. Let's refuse to deceive ourselves in practical disobedience and choose to follow the instructions found in the Book of James:

*But be doers of the word, and not hearers only, deceiving yourselves.
For if anyone is a hearer of the word and not a doer, he is like a man observing his natural face in a mirror; for he observes himself, goes away, and immediately forgets what kind of man he was. But he who looks into the perfect law of liberty and continues in it, and is not a forgetful hearer but a doer of the work, this one will be blessed in what he does. (James 1:22 - 25)*

Receive: Open your Bible and read Matthew 5:1-48.

Rejoice: Prayerfully consider the following: What areas of obedience have I been delaying? What is at the heart of my procrastination?

What steps of love and obedience do I need to take today as a result of discovering these truths regarding love, action, and obedience?

Release: As a result of these truths, what might need to change in my attitude, beliefs, and actions as it relates to the consistency of my spiritual obedience? Is there anything I'm delaying to obey as it pertains to serving others? If so, how can I change this today?

Day # 22 - A Perfect Love

Love the Lord your God with all your heart and with all your soul and with all your strength and with all your mind. (Luke 10:27)

When living things grow, no one is surprised. It means that their internal systems are working well and doing their jobs. Although not always as fast as we would like, all healthy things grow over time. Growth is essentially the result of a natural process. This process is hardwired in the DNA of living organisms and unfolded over time. You can often predict how much certain organisms will grow under controlled conditions.

God wants you to love Him by pursuing Him with your total being.

In the Christian life, love is comprehensive. It is not limited, fractional, or temporary. God loves you with a perfect love. As you continue living an abiding life, your love for God and your love for others will grow. When God connected you to His Son at the moment of salvation, you became His child forever. This relationship was intentionally designed to grow.

Are you deliberately pursuing God? He wants you to love Him by pursuing him with your total being. For this reason, God wants you to make loving him your top priority. Recognize that God is the One who has absolute control over everything. Since his provision for you through the vine can satisfy every need you have, there is no need to look elsewhere. You were designed to love and pursue God. This is a critical part of your spiritual maturity. Good spiritual health and growth depend on it.

All Your Heart   **All Your Soul**   **All Your Strength**   **All Your Mind**

As you deepen your connection to the vine, you will grow in your love, passion, and appreciation for the vinedresser. Your capacity to love increases as you maintain a constant flow to and from the vine. In other words, uninterrupted fellowship feeds your spiritual growth. This is why it is so important to confess your sins right away; unconfessed sin will always interrupt your fellowship and prevent you from loving God with 100% of your heart, soul, strength, and mind. As you continue living an abiding life, your love for God and your love for others will grow and mature.

As you deepen your connection to the vine, you will grow in your love,
passion, and appreciation for the vinedresser.

Remember the promise you have in Christ Jesus:

**If we confess our sins, he is faithful and just to forgive us our sins
and to cleanse us from all unrighteousness. If we say we have not sinned,
we make him a liar, and his word is not in us. (1 John 1:9-10)**

What things have interrupted your fellowship with God in the past? Why
are these things so attractive to you? What is the root of their power over
your life. Ask the Lord to guide you to avoid interruptions and remain in
good fellowship. Don't let your love for God stop growing in your heart,
mind, soul, and strength as a result of unconfessed sins. No matter how far
you may have traveled away from God in submission to sin, it only takes
one step, repentance, to make things right and restore the relationship.

Don't forget, if you abide more, you will sin less. We always sin more
when we abide less. We compromise our integrity and submit to more
temptations when we move away from walking in the Spirit and enjoying
life as a branch. So let's choose to abide in Christ as we live in total
submission to the Lord and in full obedience to God's Word.

As you continue living an abiding life, your love
for God and your love for others will grow.

Receive: Open your Bible and read 1 John 1:9-10.

Rejoice: Prayerfully consider the following: Am I allowing any sin to stop
my love for God from flourishing and growing as the Lord desires?

Release: What spiritual disruptors or sins do I need to be more aware of
in my daily activities and patterns of thinking? What areas need to be
strengthened? What areas need to be avoided? Is there someone
struggling with sin for me to encourage today with what I have learned?

Day # 23 - A Satisfying Love

These things I have spoken to you, that My joy may remain in you,
and that your joy may be full. (John 15:11)

When a mother agonizes in labor for several hours to deliver her new baby, it is an exhausting experience to say the least. The pain she experiences is intense and very real; yet all of this quickly fades the moment the new baby is in her arms. The joy of that precious moment surpasses the exhaustion and great pain caused by her labor.

A strong characteristic of your life should be a heart filled with joy.

You were created to enjoy God's purposes for your life. That may sound a bit strange, but it's true. God created you for a greater purpose; and there is nothing dull or common about it. A strong characteristic of your life should be a heart filled with joy. We're not talking about happiness. Happiness is temporary, but joy is eternal. Happiness depends on the measure of our circumstances and feelings.

Joy is determined by the transformation of the inner life through the power of the Holy Spirit. Joy is internal and immeasurable. Joy is produced by God and sustained by God as we abide in Christ. Our joy increases as we learn to receive, rejoice, and release God's love to others more consistently. The most joyful Christians in our world today are those who have learned to abide in Christ Jesus through long, intense, exhausting, and painful circumstances. Would that reflect your testimony today?

You must believe that God's intentions for your life are pure and good. Almighty God has a good plan for your life (Philippians 1:6). You can trust the Lord wholeheartedly with your life.

God wants you to run the Christian race with a full tank. He wants you to persevere and finish strong. The uninterrupted presence of Christ flowing through your life is the power needed to live and finish strong. Jesus is your exclusive source for abundant satisfaction. Find the strength to live from the right source, as the wrong source will deplete you spiritually. David's source helped him to persevere in times of increasing stress and hardship:

Now David was greatly distressed, for the people spoke of stoning him,
because the soul of all the people was grieved.
But David strengthened himself in the Lord his God. (1 Samuel 30:6).

All the spiritual resources you need are readily available for you to apply in your life right now. You don't have to go out and look for a temporary fix for satisfaction. You don't have to try buying more stuff to make you happy. All the satisfaction you'll ever need is already present within you in Christ Jesus. Regardless of your circumstances, you can have abundant joy right now! Don't forget: joy comes from the Lord.

The uninterrupted presence of Christ flowing through your life is the power needed to live and finish strong.

If you have a real need, ask God and watch him provide. He wants you to experience the joy found in living through the vine. Sometimes He will allow you to struggle, but trust him; it is ultimately for your good. He loves you and has a purpose for every circumstance. Enjoy the presence of the Lord at work within you. Find your joy in the Lord.

Jesus said, "Until now you have asked nothing in My name. Ask, and you will receive, that your joy may be full." (John 16:24)

Receive: Open your Bible and read 1 John 1:4.

Rejoice: Prayerfully consider the following: Is my joy full? If not, can it be that I am trying to find satisfaction in things, money, fame, or power?

Release: Would others describe my life as happy or joyful? What would people say is my source of joy? What would they say I speak about the most? Who can I tell today about the immeasurable joy found in knowing Jesus Christ?

Day # 24 - A Constant Battle

I say then: Walk in the Spirit, and you shall not fulfill the lust of the flesh.
For the flesh lusts against the Spirit, and the Spirit against the flesh;
and these are contrary to one another, so that you do not do
the things that you wish. (Galatians 5:16 - 17)

Some people avoid intense arguments while others readily welcome them. Knowing that such conflicts lead to no good end, sidestepping them is often a good choice as the intensity increases while love decreases. When you grow up in a tough neighborhood, you learn how to fight well or run fast. But what do you do when faced with a spiritual attack? Are you supposed to fight or run? How should you respond?

The desires of your flesh are in constant opposition to God's Word.

Stand and let God fight! The Christian life is a daily battle. But this battle is not against those we see everyday. This battle does not involve physical combat. Why? It is spiritual in nature. We battle against the unseen powers of darkness which influence what people say, how people think, and how they respond to those around them. Let's get ready and let God fight.

For we do not wrestle against flesh and blood, but against principalities, against
powers, against the rulers of the darkness of this age, against spiritual hosts
of wickedness in the heavenly places. Therefore take up the whole armor of God,
that you may be able to withstand in the evil day, and having done all,
to stand. (Ephesians 6:12-13)

You will be attacked from many directions, but your greatest battle will originate from within. The desires of your flesh are in constant opposition to God's Word. They never rest and they never want to lose. They won't surrender, and they won't be completely satisfied. As a child of God, you already have the power to conquer your flesh. Let God fight for you.

As you walk in the Spirit by living an abiding life,
you will win the battle over your flesh.

Live to win. As you walk in the Spirit by living an abiding life, you will win the battle over your flesh. The power of God's Spirit is always far greater than the power of the flesh. You are not in a losing battle, you are in a war that has already been won. The power to win now lives in you. No matter what destructive habits or addictions defeated you in the past, the power to overcome now lives inside you. Abiding is the way you fight back.

No matter what destructive habits or addictions defeated you in the past, the power to overcome now lives within you.

Don't feel guilty. Don't beat yourself up when you sin and lose an individual battle. Confess your sins to the Lord, get back up, and stand. Let God fight your battles for you. When you try to fight your spiritual battles in your own strength, you lose. But when you stand and allow God's mighty power to fight through you, you are sure to win. You can be confident when God is doing the fighting. He can take care of your battles.

No matter what destructive habits defeated you in the past, the power to overcome these sinful habits now lives within you. You don't have to fight what you can't see. You simply have to put on God's armor every day, stand in Christ, and watch the Lord fight for you. Paul wrote:

Finally, my brethren, be strong in the Lord and in the power of His might. Put on the whole armor of God, that you may be able to stand against the wiles of the devil. (Ephesians 6:10-11)

Receive: Open your Bible and read 1 Corinthians 10:13.

Rejoice: Prayerfully consider the following: What are the three main battles that I have struggled with in the past? Why have they been so difficult for me to overcome in the past?

Release: Have I tried winning spiritual battles without God's help? What am I learning in this devotional to change my approach? What friends of mine need to hear what I have learned to strengthen their spiritual walk?

Day # 25 - Delivering Love and Joy

But the fruit of the Spirit is love, joy. (Galatians 5:22)

You answer the doorbell and see a deliveryman on your doorstep. Before he even says a single word, you already know what he is going to deliver. The smell of pizza gives it away initially, but the uniform confirms it. You have been waiting patiently for the delivery to arrive. And now you are ready to receive what the delivery person intends to deliver.

As a Christian, demonstrating God's love to others is your most important delivery.

People are waiting expectantly for your special delivery. Are you going to do your job? What are you going to give them? What you deliver is very important. As a Christian, demonstrating God's love to others is your most important delivery. Delivering God's love is an enjoyable and fulfilling experience. God's love comes in a variety of flavors, shapes, and sizes. Every flavor of God's love is for people to enjoy and generously share with others. It is intended to remind them of the source of true love.

It is fulfilling to deliver what God designed you to deliver! However, if your delivery of God's love to others has stopped, it will negatively affect your relationship with the Lord. Your delivery of God's love to a broken world was meant to be an ongoing activity rather than a one-time event. You were designed to take God's love to others. Get started!

Every flavor of God's love is for people to enjoy and generously share with others.

God shows His love to people in many different ways. Variety is a good thing. Without variety our lives would be very dull. Did you know that a variety of fruit glorifies God? Don't try to deliver God's love in exactly the same way others do. God created you the way you are for a reason. The methods of your delivery are often shaped by your personality, but the characteristics of love remain the same. When you are walking in the Spirit, abiding in Jesus, you will identify with the following characteristics:

Love suffers long and is kind; love does not envy; love does not parade itself, is not puffed up; does not behave rudely, does not seek its own, is not provoked, thinks no evil; does not rejoice in iniquity, but rejoices in the truth; bears all things, believes all things, hopes all things, endures all things. Love never fails. And now abide faith, hope, love, these three; but the greatest of these is love. (1 Corinthians 13:4-8)

It's not about you. Why? Simply put, love is about others. There is nothing selfish about it. Delivering a joyful supply of love to others is about knowing God and making him known. You don't produce this kind of love, because it can't be manufactured. God's love is received.

As a branch, you simply receive God's love and deliver it to others with a cheerful and generous spirit. Are you generously distributing what the Lord has given you in Christ? Are you generous with your material possessions? Are you generous with your time? What about financial generosity? Is it an obvious characteristic of your life?

Delivering God's love and joy is about being a branch under complete submission to the vine and the plans of the vinedresser. You were uniquely designed to deliver God's love to others. So don't hold back and hoard God's love for yourself. Give it away freely to others. Let God multiply His love as you deliberately share God's love with others.

> You were uniquely designed to deliver God's love to others.

Receive: Open your Bible and read 1 Corinthians 13:1-8.

Rejoice: Prayerfully consider the following: Am I delivering a generous supply of love and joy to others? How can I do this more effectively?

Release: In what areas of my life do I have a tendency of hoarding and keeping things for myself? What characteristics of God's love do I enjoy sharing with others the most? Find someone today and continue sharing God's love in a generous and gracious way.

Abiding Thoughts

No church lacks anything. Having Jesus, they have all they need to succeed.
They must improve their receiving, not their doing.

There are no bad places for a church to exist.
There are only places where great receivers must be present.

The church needs to go in the direction of pain
if we are going where Jesus is going.

Success is taking love's next step.
It is moving forward with an open heart toward God and man.

Perfection is living with a heart open like God's.

Everything and everyone must be seen through Jesus' eyes
and treated according to His intentions.

The goal is God's glory.

When His character is made perfectly visible and available, all will be well.

A healthy church is one in which every branch is experiencing
true satisfaction in the vine and releasing that satisfaction
without hesitation or judging.

I sin when I seek satisfaction apart from the vine.

Day # 26 - Peace and Longsuffering

But the fruit of the Spirit is love, joy, peace, longsuffering. (Galatians 5:22)

Do you have increasing stress in your life? Stress has been linked as a significant contributing factor in heart disease, mental illness, insomnia, and other health challenges. No one goes to the doctor to request more stress in their prescription. When it comes to stress, more is definitely not better. Stress makes things worse. It negatively accelerates specific health problems. Stress gives you more of what you don't want and faster.

Stress and peace were not designed to coexist. God's peace displaces stress and helps us to find true inner peace within our spirit, soul, and mind. People desperately need to experience peace. They need to find real peace for their spirit and find rest for their mind and soul. For the Christian, we do not have to hunt in pursuit of inner peace. Jesus Christ is our eternal peace. The Lord gives us peace from within. Moreover, the Lord teaches us how to live at peace with others and become peacemakers.

You don't have to search for peace. You already have it.

The world desperately wants lasting peace but can't find it. God's infinite peace lives within every believer. The presence of Christ is ready to help you successfully navigate through the storms of life and experience the peace of God. You don't have to search for peace, because you already have it. As you find others defeated by the storms of life, point them to God's perfect refuge, God's eternal peace, which is found in the person of Jesus Christ. Jesus said to His disciples:

Peace I leave with you, My peace I give to you; not as the world gives do I give to you. Let not your heart be troubled, neither let it be afraid. (John 14:27)

Anxiety should no longer control your thinking. As God's child, you can be confident of God's provision in every area of your life. Develop the habit of seeking the Lord's provision for all of your needs. He is able, more than able, to take care of you. Likewise, the Lord is more than able to take care of those around you. With each opportunity, boldly share how God has graciously provided for your needs. The Apostle Paul reminds us:

Be anxious for nothing, but in everything by prayer and supplication, with thanksgiving let your requests be made known to God; and the peace of God, which surpasses all understanding will guard your hearts and minds through Christ Jesus. (Philippians 4:6 - 7)

Don't be surprised if you find yourself in the middle of a perfect storm. The vinedresser may decide to place you right in the middle of a physical, relational, or financial crisis. Why would He allow this? He may decide to use you to model the abiding life and serve as an encouragement to branches nearby. But don't worry, the Lord can deliver an abundance of fruit as He leads you through the storms of life. Paul wrote:

I, therefore, the prisoner of the Lord, beseech you to walk worthy of the calling with which you were called, with all lowliness and gentleness, with longsuffering, bearing with one another in love, endeavoring to keep the unity of the Spirit in the bond of peace. (Ephesians 4:1-3)

You don't have to search for peace. You already have it.

Receive: Open your Bible and read Matthew 6:25.

Rejoice: Prayerfully consider the following: Am I being honest with God about my worries, fears, and anxieties? What difficulties and areas of increasing stress am I neglecting to bring before Him?

Release: What people has God placed around me that need to hear about God's eternal peace in Jesus? How can I encourage them today to take one step of faith and get closer to the Savior?

Day # 27 - Kindness, Goodness, and Faithfulness

But the fruit of the Spirit is love, joy, peace, longsuffering, kindness, goodness, faithfulness. (Galatians 5:22)

There are certain ingredients you look for before preparing a special meal. Whether you're following a recipe or operating with the instincts of a seasoned cook, you know the importance of finding exactly what you need to make that special dish a success. Every time you use these ingredients the right taste is guaranteed. Predictability in preparing an important meal is a good thing. Experimenting in the unknown is risky. It is a great feeling to know the predictability of the right ingredients.

You were designed to deliver kindness by helping others find rest. As a Christian, your life should be marked by kindness. Delivering kindness means removing the burdens others are carrying; it means simultaneously lightening the weights of life and giving others an opportunity to rest. We know that people are stressed and tired, but what are we doing about it?

Jesus said, "Come to Me, all you who labor and are heavy laden, and I will give you rest. Take My yoke upon you and learn from Me, for I am gentle and lowly in heart, and you will find rest for your souls." (Matthew 11:28 - 29)

Kindness also means showing mercy and favor to others, even when you don't think they deserve it. If you wait to receive kindness from others before delivering kindness, you may wait for a very long time. The kindness given freely to you in Christ should serve to motivate you sharing God's kindness with others. We need to give kindness to give kindness rather than give kindness to receive kindness. We've already received the kindness of God. And God's kindness is far more than what we needed.

Check your motives. Your delivery is to be wrapped in purity. Goodness has to do with being whole and pure. Every demonstration of God's love should be delivered with complete integrity. Integrity means being one, whole, or complete. There are no mixed messages, ulterior motives, or deceit. Every opportunity you have to deliver God's love is to be characterized by a pure heart. Even when you don't see immediate results, practice moral excellence and let God take care of the results. Do good to all and live in complete integrity. The Apostle Paul wrote:

"And let us not grow weary while doing good, for in due season we shall reap if we do not lose heart. Therefore, as we have opportunity, let us do good to all, especially to those who are of the household of faith" (Galatians 6:9-10).

Every demonstration of God's love should be delivered with complete integrity.

Faithfulness matters to God! Can your family, friends, neighbors and co-workers count on you? Or have you been known to say one thing and then do another instead? If so, that old behavior was not buried when Jesus moved into your life. Go ahead and bury it now in repentance to your Savior. God wants you to be a faithful steward in every area of your life. This includes relationships, work, body, mind, finances, and others.

Being faithful has a totally different look and feel. In Christ, you can live responsibly. God expects you to be faithful. You now have the capacity to deliver truth consistently, faithfully. You no longer need to blame others for your actions. And in the process, you can teach believers around you what you have learned and obeyed (2 Timothy 2:2). Faithfulness may not be popular, but it is certainly Biblical. The Lord will reward the faithful. This is the consistent teaching of God's Word. Show genuine kindness, practice goodness, and be faithful in all things through the power of God's Spirit.

Receive: Open your Bible and read John 8-11. Ask the Lord to speak to you as you read, follow, and practice God's Word.

Rejoice: Prayerfully consider the following: What are three ways that Jesus delivered kindness and goodness to others? How can I do likewise?

1.

2.

3.

Receive: As a result of these truths, what might need to change in my attitude, beliefs, and actions as it relates to practicing kindness, goodness, and faithfulness? What practical steps should I start with?

Day # 28 - Gentleness and Self-Control

But the fruit of the Spirit is love, joy, peace, longsuffering, kindness, goodness, faithfulness, gentleness, self-control. Against such there is no law. And those who are Christ's have crucified the flesh with its passions and desires. If we live in the Spirit, let us also walk in the Spirit. Let us not become conceited, provoking one another, envying one another. (Galatians 5:22 - 26)

The customer yells, "I'll have one more drink, Sam," as he throws his glass on the floor. He's a regular at the bar. Everyone knows this unruly customer. Although often polite when sober, his lack of self-control transforms him into an irresponsible monster after drinking for two hours. It is a difficult sight to see. His words and actions have become destructive.

Living an abiding life determines both the quality and the quantity of your gentleness.

Delivering gentleness is anything but normal. It isn't something we see every day. Often, we experience the exact opposite from those around us. Delivering gentleness involves humbling yourself before God and remaining submissive to His ways. Living an abiding life determines both the quality and the quantity of your gentleness. Remember, the vine is the One who produces the fruit. Abiding in Christ and being a good receiver, is a prerequisite to producing lasting gentleness. James wrote:

Therefore lay aside all filthiness and overflow of wickedness, and receive with meekness the implanted word, which is able to save your souls. But be doers of the word, and not hearers only, deceiving yourselves. (James 1:21 - 22)

Delivering gentleness means leading instead of forcing, guiding instead of demanding, and being considerate instead of uncaring. Delivering gentleness involves receiving instructions cheerfully and maintaining the right attitude. It means demonstrating a caring spirit and taking the time to serve and help others without expecting anything in return.

People need to know that you really care about them. Do you genuinely love and care about others? Are you forceful, rough, and inconsiderate towards others? Are you a demanding person, insisting on always getting what you want and when you want it? Do the words patient, caring, understanding and thoughtful escape your spiritual profile? If they do, you're in trouble, big trouble. The fruit of the Spirit is gentleness. Therefore, gentleness should serve as a strong characteristic of our spiritual profile in Christ. It should be visible and ongoing in our lives.

Paul reminds us:

And be kind to one another, tenderhearted, forgiving one another, even as God in Christ forgave you. (Ephesians 4:32)

You cannot live an abiding life in Christ and lack self-control at the same time. Where Christ dwells as Lord, self-control is present. When you are walking in the Spirit you will display and deliver self-control. Food, spending, alcohol, and sexual temptations are common areas requiring the Spirit's control. When the flesh is in control, we lose control in these areas and submit to the flesh. This is evidence that we are not abiding.

However, when we walk in the Spirit, abide, we won't respond as others do. We won't participate in activities or conversations that destroy others or feed the desires of our flesh. Walking in the Spirit and exercising self-control work together. Gentleness and self-control are products of the Holy Spirit, not the flesh. Gentleness and self-control are the fruit of an abiding life. Keep learning from God's Word and let God's Spirit continue shaping your life as you abide in Christ more each day.

When you're walking in the Spirit you will display and deliver self-control.

Receive: Open your Bible and read Galatians 5:1-26.

Rejoice: Prayerfully consider the following: Where are gentleness and self-control lacking in my life? What is the root cause for this shortage?

Release: As a result of these truths, what might need to change in my attitude, beliefs, and actions regarding self-control and gentleness?

Day # 29 - Identify and Engage

For this reason the Jews persecuted Jesus, and sought to kill Him, because He had
done these things on the Sabbath. But Jesus answered them, 'My Father has been
working until now, and I have been working.' Therefore the Jews sought all the
more to kill Him, because He not only broke the Sabbath, but also said that God was
His Father, making Himself equal with God. Then Jesus answered and said to them,
'Most assuredly, I say to you, the Son can do nothing of Himself, but what He sees
the Father do; for whatever He does, the Son also does in like manner.
For the Father loves the Son, and shows Him all things that He Himself does;
and He will show Him greater works than these, that you may marvel.
(John 5:16 - 20)

Do you enjoy finding, catching, and eating fish? If so, using the right kind
of bait is essential for catching the right fish. Part of good fishing involves
identifying what kind of fish you want to catch and knowing where to find
them. This leads to the question, "What do these fish love to eat?" The
answer to this question helps you identify and engage these fish more
precisely. And the best part is when you can enjoy your catch at dinner.

God wants you to be dynamically
involved in His work of changing lives.

God, the vinedresser, is always at work around you. His work of life-
transformation is alive and well. This great work takes place with those you
come in contact with every day. The Lord leads us to identify and engage
people without Christ. There are many good activities in life to get
involved in. God wants you to be dynamically involved in his work of
changing lives. And spiritual fishing is an important part of his great work.

The Christian life is not about staying busy and joining multiple ministries
at church. It's about living through the vine and helping others realize this
same connection in their lives. We have to be intentional with our time
and with our resources. Changing lives and transforming families is well
worth our investment to time, energy, and resources.

Identify and engage. God's desire is to magnify His name through your
life as you identify his work and get involved. Participating in God's work
is the most exciting adventure you'll ever embark on. Living through the
vine is critical in this process. God's work needs to be carried out in God's
power. He is the one who leads people to repentance and faith in Christ.
As you learn to hear God's voice, see where God is working, and respond
to his ways, your capacity to engage in His work significantly increases.

As you come in contact with others this week, prayerfully consider these questions as you speak with them:

- How does the Lord want me to encourage them today?
- Is there a specific need in their life I can pray for?
- How can I use my gifts, talents, skills, and abilities to serve them?
- How can I express just how much God loves them?
- How can I express just how much I care about their soul?
- How can I deliver God's love to them in a meaningful way?

Ask the Lord to help you identify His work and then respond to His lead. Get involved with what God is doing. Since the Lord is always at work, it's not difficult to identify where God is working and engage others. Get ready to identify and engage those who need hope and respond as the Lord leads you. Get ready to experience the ride of your life in Christ!

As you learn to hear God's voice and respond to His ways, your capacity to engage in God's work increases.

Receive: Open your Bible and read 1 Peter 2:17. What practical application do you observe in this text for you to follow.

Rejoice: Prayerfully consider the following: Am I honoring others by identifying their needs and serving them unconditionally? Do I often assume the attitude of a servant, willing and available to serve others in selfless love?

Release: Do I identify and engage people who don't know Christ regularly in conversation? What stops me from engaging more with those who need to know the Savior?

Day # 30 - Finish the work

*I have glorified You on the earth. I have finished the work
which You have given Me to do.* (John 17:1-4)

We all love a great finish as in a good movie. The intensity of a final scene can move people physically and emotionally. At times we are moved to tears and sighs of relief and at other times, thunderous applause. We gladly cheer for the victory of the unsung hero and celebrate the defeat of the notorious villain. There is nothing quite like a great finish.

God loves to watch a great finish in the lives of His people. He loves to see lives transformed by his awesome power. God loves to see relationships healed and marriages restored. He loves to see the widow find support and the orphan find a home. God loves to see forgiveness demonstrated and mercy distributed through his people. God loves to see His great work accomplished through your life too. He wants to see you thrive and finish well. Commit today to finish God's mission and work through your life!

God loves to watch a great finish in the lives of His people.

God wants you to finish the work He ordained for you to do. He wants you to persevere and make a difference in the lives of those around you. He wants you to finish your race without being disqualified. You are in a race that only you can run. Keep running to God as your source. Keep receiving from the vine. Keep abiding every morning, afternoon, and evening. The Apostle Paul wrote to young Timothy:

*I have fought the good fight, I have finished the race, I have kept the faith.
Finally, there is laid up for me the crown of righteousness, which the Lord,
the righteous Judge, will give to me on that Day, and not to me only
but also to all who have loved His appearing.* (2 Timothy 4:7-8)

The vinedresser is counting on you to deliver His love and get the job done. He has invested heavily in your life and He is looking forward to a generous return. Remember, the enemy wants to destroy your life. Satan doesn't want you to finish the work. He will do everything he can, and even use other branches to discourage you along the way. Don't get sidetracked...finish the work. Stay focused...finish the work. Don't get discouraged...finish the work. This is your calling. John reminds us:

He [Jesus] who is in you is greater than he who is in the world. (1 John 4:4)

Living an abiding life is the way to end well and finish God's great work. Remember, abiding is simply spending time with Jesus and responding to His instructions moment-by-moment as you receive, rejoice, and release God's love to those around you. This is the key to glorifying God, bearing fruit, and fulfilling God's purposes for your life.

Spend time today thanking God for helping you continue His work through your life. Continue studying God's Word and receiving from His Son each and every day. Let God finish His great work through you, through abiding. This is how He designed for you to grow in your faith. This is how the Lord desires for you to live day-by-day and moment-by-moment. Pace yourself. You're in a race and you need to finish well to win. Finish your race; finish the work God has called you to do.

God wants you to finish the work He chose you to do.

Receive: Open your Bible and read 1 Peter 2:17.

Rejoice: Prayerfully consider the following: Am I finishing what God is asking me to do? Am I persevering in my love and service to others? Am I pacing myself by avoiding extremes and remaining in Christ?

Release: What is potentially the biggest obstacle that will try to prevent me from finishing my race well? What can I do practically to overcome this obstacle and persevere to victory?

Abiding Thoughts

The Christian life is as simple as receive, rejoice, release.
It is as simple as receiving from Jesus what He is ready,
willing and able to give, enjoying now what he is giving
and releasing to others what has been received
because there is more where that came from.

Jesus was behaving naturally 100% of the time.
His essence was so at peace with the Father that his effort
and effect always revealed God's glory.

Every church can have perfect health, produce much fruit and become a vineyard
full of abiding branches glorifying God.

As a branch in the vine, my concern should be the vine, not the fruit.
The vinedresser will watch for the fruit he wants
and do all the pruning necessary to produce it.

The greatest compliment I pay to God each day
is to show up empty and ask.

Being perfect is always about right now. I am perfect moment by moment
and that is only possible if God's moment by moment perfection
flows from His open heart through my open heart.

One simple question can inform my behavior toward people in sin:
"How should we who will never die treat those who may never live?"

What's Next?

But also for this very reason, giving all diligence, add to your faith virtue, to virtue knowledge, to knowledge self-control, to self-control perseverance, to perseverance godliness, to godliness brotherly kindness, and to brotherly kindness love. For if these things are yours and abound, you will be neither barren nor unfruitful in the knowledge of our Lord Jesus Christ. (2 Peter 1:5-8).

What's next for you? The answer may surprise you. You don't have to digest two to three Christian books per week, listen to Christian radio 24/7, or add several new activities to your schedule. The next step is to simply build on the foundation already laid over this last year: read, reflect, and respond. Your daily spiritual nourishment will vary, but the source will remain the same. The vinedresser will work through the vine to shape your life for greater impact. Get ready for God to work in you and through you!

Branches don't change what they're doing to grow and bear fruit. They do however change certain characteristics about themselves as new nutrients are introduced from the vine. Now is the time for you to know the Lord more intimately by adding to this way of life, the abiding life, rather than replacing it with a totally new one. Your old nature was designed to die and be replaced, but your new nature was designed to live and grow generously. How can you continue growing in your faith? Remember the main goal. **You were designed to glorify God by bearing much fruit.**

You grow in your faith by bearing fruit. As you grow spiritually, you will bear more fruit. Here are some questions for you to consider as you build on the foundation of an abiding life:

- What changes are still pending for me to make to wholeheartedly follow God's Word?
- What spiritual deliveries to others are on hold?
- What changes to my schedule need to happen to help me spend more time in prayer, outreach, Bible study, and small groups?

Here are some additional questions for you to consider:

- What other books of the Bible would be best for me to study next and who can coach me along the way?
- What class or small group do I need to attend to help increase my love for God, His word, His people, and others?

Make daily sacrifices to grow your faith. Remember the words of Jesus,

And anyone who does not carry his cross and follow me cannot be my disciple. (Luke 14:27)

The One Anothers

Build healthy relationships with God's people

Stop grumbling about one another (John 6:43)

Love one another just as Jesus has loved you (John 13:34)

Overflow with love for one another (1 Thessalonians 3:13)

Overflow with love for everyone (1 Thessalonians 3:13)

Love one another with brotherly affection (Romans 12:10)

Outdo one another in showing honor (Romans 12:10)

Love one another (1 John 3:11)

Be of the same mind toward one another (Romans 12:16)

Accept one another in love (Ephesians 4:1-3)

Be united in Spirit with one another (Ephesians 4:1-3)

Be kind to one another (Ephesians 4:32)

Be tenderhearted to one another (Ephesians 4:32)

The One Anothers

Build healthy relationships with God's people

Forgive one another just as God in Christ also has forgiven you
(Ephesians 4:32)

Do not lie to one another (Colossians 3:9)

Bear with one another from the heart (Colossians 3:13)

Do not complain about one another (James 5:9)

Be at peace with one another (Mark 9:50)

Do not judge one another (Romans 14:13)

Through love, serve one another (Galatians 5:13)

Stop fighting with one another (Galatians 5:15)

Carry one another's burdens (Galatians 6:2)

Submit to one another out of reverence for Christ (Ephesians 5:21)

Pursue the things which make for peace with one another
(Romans 14:19)

Pursue the things which build up one another (Romans 14:19)

The One Anothers

Build healthy relationships with God's people

Be like-minded toward one another (Romans 15:5-7)

Receive one another, just as Christ also received you (Romans 15:5-7)

Encourage one another daily (Hebrews 3:12)

Stimulate one another to love and practice good works (Hebrews 10:24-25)

Encourage one another (Hebrews 10:24-25)

Teach and admonish one another with all wisdom (Colossians 3:16)

Clothe yourselves, all of you, with humility toward one another (1 Peter 5:5)

Wash one another's feet (John 13:14)

Submit to one another (Ephesians 5:21)

Be united in thought with one another (Philippians 2:1-4)

Have the same love for one another (Philippians 2:1-4)

The One Anothers

Build healthy relationships with God's people

Consider one another more important than yourself (Philippians 2:1-4)

Look out for the interests of one another (Philippians 2:1-4)

In humility, consider one another (Philippians 2:1-4)

Encourage one another (1 Thessalonians 5:11)

Build up one another (1 Thessalonians 5:11)

Be hospitable to one another without complaining (1 Peter 4:9)

Serve one another (1 Peter 4:10)

Confess your sins to one another (James 5:16)

Pray for one another (James 5:16)

Made in the USA
Middletown, DE
05 February 2023

24115607R00056